EXPLORING

HYPERMEDIA

PHILIP BARKER

KOGAN
PAGE

Published in association with the AETT

To Alix and Hannah

The Educational and Training Technology Series

Series Editor: Chris Bell
Exploring Hypermedia Philip Barker
Successful Instructional Diagrams Ric Lowe

First published in 1993

Kogan Page Limited
120 Pentonville Road
London N1 9JN

British Library Cataloguing in Publication Data

A CIP record for this book is available from the British Library

ISBN 0 7494 0946 0

Typeset by BookEns Ltd., Baldock, Herts.
Printed and bound in Great Britain by
Biddles Ltd, Guildford and King's Lynn

Contents

Figures

Tables

Series Editor's Foreword

This series is designed to help those working in all areas of education and training apply the ideas of educational and training technology in order to produce the most effective and efficient instruction. The books are also appropriate for students studying education and training.

'Education and training technology', the overall theme of this series, is a much misunderstood (or not understood) phrase. In his book *The Concept of Educational Technology* (published in 1970 by Weidenfeld and Nicolson, London) Kenneth Richmond takes some 70 pages to discuss the meaning of the phrase. Numerous other authors have also spent many pages discussing the ideas from both conceptual and practical viewpoints. Definitions, often conflicting, abound.

It is my belief that the most valuable way of considering educational and training technology is to think in terms of:

- the technology *of* education and training, and
- the use of technologies *in* education and training.

The former, the less tangible, is very much a cross-disciplinary activity, drawing on anthropology, communications theory, learning theory, media research, psychology, sociology, statistics and many more areas. The latter is much more about the applications of hardware and software to the learning process.

In both cases, the focus is on increasing the quality (embracing both effectiveness and efficiency) of learning. Educational and training technology is concerned with the design, evaluation and assessment of the teaching and learning process (note the essential use of the term 'learning'). It is concerned with systematically analysing learning needs, relating those to relevant theories (and none too theoretically-based knowledge!) with the intention of optimizing learning. It is a rational, problem-solving approach to the needs and issues of education and training.

At its best, application of the ideas of educational and training technology is central to the improvement of education and training; to meeting the needs of learners and to fitting the 'system' to these needs. Together, the books in the series will help you do this, both from the perspective of the technology of education and training, and the use of technologies *in* education and training.

The application of computers to the processes of teaching and learning holds many promises. Their use has been seen as a way of improving the quality of delivery, increasing the individualization of learning, encouraging learner autonomy and, amongst others, providing a cost effective solution to the issue of increasing numbers of students, particularly in higher education. Imposing claims which some would refute, citing the large amounts of time, effort and finance, which, to date, seem to have produced few real results. But the technology is still new and is fast developing, its applications are newer, and those who have the vision and foresight to successfully apply the technology to real learning situations are still rather few and far between.

Of all the possible applications of computer technology to learning, hypermedia seems to be one with a great potential. It is non-linear; learning is very often non-linear; it involves the presentation of material using a variety of media, most quality learning uses a variety of media; it allows flexible and differing uses by the learner, learning is optimized when the learner can attune the 'system' to his or her needs and preferred learning styles; it facilitates feedback to the learner, quality learning requires quality feedback.

In no way is this an exhaustive list, but it should be sufficient to encourage you to dip into Philip Barker's book and to start to realize the potential of hypermedia. The book is about both the technology *of* education and training, and the use of technologies *in* education and training and, therefore, admirably meets my earlier criteria of being a valuable way of considering educational and training technology in order to improve learning.

Chris Bell
University of Plymouth

This series is commissioned by the Association of Educational and Training Technology.

Preface

Conventional approaches to the delivery of information most often adopt a basically linear form of presentation. A book, for example, consists of a series of chapters, each of which may be further subdivided into a sequence of pages. Pages are in turn organized into paragraphs and sentences, each sentence being a linear collection of words. Most conventional books (other than reference and text books) are designed in such a way that a reader would commence reading at the first page of Chapter 1 and then progress through the remaining pages before commencing on Chapter 2. Chapters 1 and 2 would usually need to be completed before subsequent chapters are processed. A video tape presentation provides another example of an essentially linear mechanism of information delivery. A viewer would normally start watching a video programme at the beginning and would then proceed sequentially (frame by frame) through to the end of the tape.

Over the last decade there have been considerable advances in the ways in which information can be stored, processed and delivered. Of particular importance are the developments that have taken place in computer storage technologies and the various mechanisms by which people can interact with computer systems. These developments have meant that large volumes of information can now be stored and displayed in 'electronic form'. Such information can be organized in a linear fashion (similar to those described above) or it can be organized into other, more sophisticated, non-linear structures. Non-linear arrangements of textual material are called 'hypertext'. Similarly, non-linear arrangements of multimedia information (combinations of text, pictures and sound) are known as 'hypermedia'. Essentially, this book is concerned with this latter category of information. *Exploring*

Hypermedia is intended to provide a description of some of the various approaches to developing and using non-linearly organized multimedia information. Special emphasis is given to educational and training applications of hypermedia techniques.

Hypertext and hypermedia have grown substantially in importance during the last ten years, mainly because of the many new mechanisms of information storage, access and delivery that they offer. This growth of importance has been paralleled by a rise in interest among teachers, lecturers, instructors and courseware designers in the use of these important techniques for teaching and learning. This book has been produced to answer some of the questions associated with the growing curiosity about hypermedia techniques and how they can be employed in pedagogic applications.

In order to 'set the scene' for subsequent chapters, the historical prelude presented in Chapter 1 outlines the 'principle of interrelatedness' upon which hypermedia is based. It then reviews some of the important developments that have taken place over the last few decades. Current developments in hypermedia technology are discussed and some possible future directions of development are then outlined. The final part of the chapter is used to draw conclusions and to summarize the way in which the remainder of the book 'unfolds'.

Chapter 2 deals with some of the technical issues of hypermedia systems. It covers these in much more detail than could be done in Chapter 1. This chapter explains in more depth the nature of 'reactive', non-linear information structures and how they can be created (using links) and accessed (using buttons). Basic methods and techniques for creating hypertext and hypermedia structures are then presented. Accessing knowledge held in non-linear information structures usually involves some form of 'navigation'. Some techniques to facilitate the navigation of hypermedia information spaces, and problems associated with their use, are then discussed. Brief consideration is also given to the different types of support tool that need to be provided for both authors and users of hypermedia systems.

Chapter 3 is concerned primarily with authoring environments – that is, tools that will facilitate the design and creation of hypermedia resources. Several different types of design tool, such as concept mapping packages, and authoring environments (for example, Guide, HyperCard and KnowledgePro) are briefly reviewed. Many authoring environments are based upon an 'object oriented' approach to design and implementation. Because of its importance, this technique is described and some of its advantages discussed. Two other important topics that are included in this chapter are: design considerations, such as conceptualization, information mapping, chunking and linking; and storage and delivery technologies – magnetic and optical disc.

The educational perspective presented in Chapter 4 describes how hypermedia techniques might be used to facilitate learning and training activities. Various types of instructional application of hypermedia are discussed. Consideration is also given to some of the ways in which this approach to instruction is able to support various styles and modes of learning based upon the use of different types of navigation metaphor. An important part of this chapter is the set of illustrative case studies that it contains. These cover such topics as flexible learning, distance learning and the design of electronic performance support systems.

One important navigation metaphor for handling large volumes of electronic information is the 'electronic book'. In recent years much importance has been attached to books that are published in electronic form – particularly those which embed hypermedia information. Such books, however, are just one of many different types of electronic book that currently exist. Other types are discussed in the taxonomies that this chapter contains. Because of their importance, the design, creation and application of hypermedia electronic books forms the essential substance of Chapter 5.

In the final chapter of the book an attempt is made to identify some of the important aspects of hypermedia that are likely to influence the future directions of its development. The issues and techniques that are discussed include virtual reality and cyberspace, intelligent hypermedia, portability issues, parallelism, and distributed hypermedia. The chapter concludes with a prediction of some future possibilities for the application and development of hypermedia methods.

Philip Barker
Professor of Applied Computing
University of Teesside, UK

1 Historical Prelude

Introduction – the basic concept

The world in which we exist consists of many different types of object. Some of these objects may have a permanent existence while others may be of a more transitory nature. Indeed, the existence of some objects may be so transitory that they might easily escape our observation.

Bearing this in mind, two basic classes of object can be readily identified: physical and abstract. Those which we perceive directly with our senses or with the aid of some mechanism of observation (such as a telescope or a microscope) are referred to as 'physical objects'. Examples of this major class include: trees, people, houses, motorcars, computers, rivers and so on. Abstract objects are more difficult to perceive. Our knowledge of this class of object is usually gained through conversation with others, reading, listening, learning, interpreting and reflecting upon events or situations in which we become involved. Typical examples of abstract objects include concepts (such as numeracy, language and religion), thoughts, relationships and ideas.

Fortunately for us, the majority of objects of which our world is composed are not organized in a chaotic or random way. Indeed, both the physical and the abstract types of object that were discussed above are very often highly structured. This structuring of objects is brought about by the nature of the 'relationships' that exist between them. Relationships are special types of object that act as a 'binding agent'; they can be used to bond together simple, primitive objects so as to form ones that have a more complex, composite structure. Depending upon the different types of relationship that exist (and their similarities one to another) objects have been classified into many different types of taxonomic grouping. Typical taxonomies include: animate – inanimate; static – dynamic; atomic – composite and so on.

As suggested above, relationships themselves form another very important class of object since they are able to add structure to a system (a system is defined here as being some collection of objects that is of interest to us). Indeed, the system structure that we perceive often depends critically upon the nature of the various relationships that we are able to deduce. Quite often different viewers of a system will perceive it in very different ways depending upon the importance of the particular objects and relationships that they identify. This situation is depicted

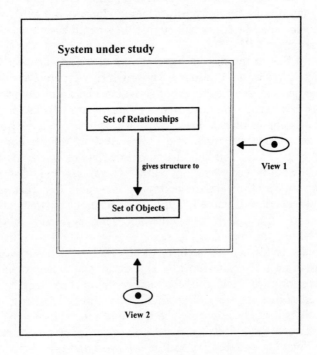

Figure 1.1 *Different views of a system*

schematically in Figure 1.1. Each viewer of the system shown in this diagram sees it according to a different 'view'. The view comprises the set of objects that are deemed to be important and the nature of the relationships that exist between these objects (Barker and Proud, 1987).

An example of a view of a system is illustrated schematically in Figure 1.2. This depicts some of the different types of object that might exist within a 'library system'. It also shows some of the various relationships that might exist between the different 'literary' objects from which libraries and their contents are composed (books, chapters, pictures, sentences, words and so on). The model depicted in this figure is by no means complete or comprehensive. It does, however, serve to illustrate the subtle distinction between basic objects and relationships. Objects are shown in capitals while

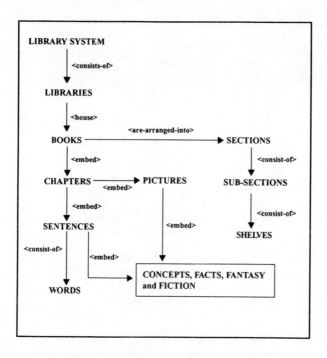

Figure 1.2 *Examples of relationships between objects*

relationships (denoted by arrows) are labelled with small letters; the name of a relationship is also enclosed in angular brackets.

A fundamental premise that has been adopted in writing this book is that all objects which exist and of which we are aware are in some way or another related to each other. How strongly any given set of objects is related depends upon the nature and strength of the relationships that exist between them. Of course, in some situations multiple relationships might exist between a particular group of objects, thereby leading to quite complex composite structures. Some of these ideas are depicted schematically in Figure 1.3. In this diagram the strength of the relationships that exist between any two objects is depicted by the boldness of the arrow(s) that denote their 'binding' relationships.

This idea of objects being related to each other is sometimes

Universe of Discourse

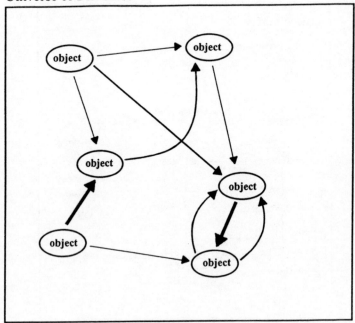

Figure 1.3 *The principle of interrelatedness*

referred to as the 'principle of interrelatedness'. Of course, in order to simplify the various systems that we study we may choose to omit from consideration any relationships which are deemed to be 'very weak'. This implies that objects that depend only upon weak relationships may also be omitted from consideration. Often, the importance that is attached to a relationship will depend upon the prevailing situation and upon the characteristics of the observer(s) of the system concerned. This gives rise to the idea of multiple views of a system which was illustrated in Figure 1.1.

In this book we shall be primarily concerned with the interrelatedness of multimedia objects (such as units of text, pictures and sound), experiences (as might be produced within cyberspace environments) and the people who are involved in creating, developing and/or using these objects. Historically, units of text were one of the first types of object to be considered in this way. Items of text (words, sentences, paragraphs, chapters, books and so on) that are interrelated in a fashion similar to that shown in Figure 1.3 are referred to as hypertext. Of course, similar forms of interrelatedness can exist between pictorial forms (hyperimages) and elements of sound (hypersound). Multimedia objects that are related in this way are referred to by the term 'hypermedia'.

Major milestones

Over the last few decades considerable attention has been devoted to research and development of hypertext and hypermedia systems. In order to set the scene for the topics that are discussed in subsequent chapters, the remainder of this section attempts to identify and briefly describe some of the important historical milestones of developments in this area. No claim is made with respect to the comprehensiveness of the material that is presented; the treatment that is given is intended to be representative rather than definitive of the work that has been undertaken.

Vanevar Bush and the memex (1945)

The basic concepts underlying hypertext and hypermedia were first formulated and published nearly 50 years ago (in 1945) by Vanevar Bush. Bush, who was the director of the US Government's Office of Scientific Research and Development, wrote an article in which he described his vision of a knowledge-handling tool (called 'the memex') in which individuals could store vast quantities of information. The memex would allow the creation of personal links between items of information and would use associative indexing to facilitate information retrieval (Bush, 1945). Although the technology to construct the memex was not really available in 1945, the ideas put forward by Bush form the basis of the hypertext systems that we use today.

Engelbart and the Augment system (1962)

During his research career at Stanford Research Institute in the USA, Douglas Engelbart and his colleagues invented and developed a wide range of computer-related products such as the mouse, electronic mail and on-line help systems. Many of the products were developed as a result of the fundamental research that was being undertaken in the Augmentation Research Laboratory (ARL) during the period 1962 to 1975 (Engelbart and English, 1968). The ARL was dedicated to the development of tools that would 'augment human intelligence'. Undoubtedly, within this theme, one of Engelbart's most important achievements was the development of the first operational and usable hypertext system – 'Augment' (Engelbart, 1963; 1984).

Augment was implemented on a central mainframe computer and used a database facility to hold all the common files that were embedded within the system. Each 'knowledge worker' with access to the system accessed his or her personal workspace by means of a workstation attached to the central time-sharing computer. Augment, like other early hypertext systems (see below), emphasized three basic features: a database of non-linear text; 'view filters' which selected information from the database; and 'views' which structured the display of the information for the particular workstation being used. The Augment system is still available commercially and is distributed today by the McDonnell Douglas Corporation.

Ted Nelson and Xanadu (1965)

The terms 'hypertext' and 'hypermedia' were first introduced by Theodore Nelson who defined hypertext as being: 'computer supported non-sequential writing' (Nelson, 1967). Nelson had a visionary idea (which he called 'Xanadu') of a 'docuverse' containing all the world's literature interlinked in various ways in order to support multiple users and multiple applications. According to Nelson (1980), Xanadu was a plan for:

> a worldwide network intended to serve hundreds of millions of users simultaneously from the corpus of the world's stored writings, graphics and data ... It is a design for a new literature and a system of order to make such a network understandable, usable and readily expansible to any degree.

Xanadu was not a large centralized software system but rather an idea for software running a decentralized network. It was a concept for a storage system that would permit documents to be stored only once in a 'universal data structure' to which all other documents could be mapped. From the point of view of authoring, Nelson envisaged that Xanadu would permit: 1) the allocation of credit for authorship and publishing; 2) the allocation of payment of royalties based upon readers' use of documents; and 3) quotability of any documents with easy tracing to the source of quotations by means of hypertext links.

Brown University and instructional applications (1968)

Brown University in the USA was one of the first organizations to study and apply the use of hypertext for instructional purposes. Much of the development work in this area was undertaken by the Institute for Research and Scholarship (IRIS) — a team of research workers led by Andries van Dam. One of the most important outcomes of the work at Brown University was the development of the Intermedia system — an authoring tool to support the design and development of multimedia and hypermedia documents that were capable of incorporating text, line diagrams and video disc segments (Meyrowitz, 1986; Yankelovich *et al.*, 1985). An important aspect of the Intermedia system was its 'web' structure. Webs provide a way of making hypertext and hypermedia links context-dependent.

The Intermedia system was designed for use by college professors in order to organize and present material and for students to create reports. Students can also browse through material and add their own notes and annotations. During the early 1970s hypertext systems were used at Brown University to support the teaching of a range of subjects such as English poetry, cell biology and English literature. Evaluation of the effects of hypertext in teaching revealed that the use of the Intermedia system could result in a deeper understanding of the material taught. Indeed, not only did students do better in term assessments, but it is claimed that they actually read more conventional publications and were more confident in seminars (Landow, 1989a).

Carnegie-Mellon University: the ZOG group and KMS (1972)

In addition to the work that was undertaken by the IRIS group at Brown University, many other academic research groups were also making significant early contributions to the development of hypertext and hypermedia. Some of the most important of these were made at Carnegie-Mellon University in Pittsburgh, USA. A group of researchers at this university (Newell, McCracken, Akscyn and Robertson) were actively developing a group of hypertext systems collectively known by the name of 'ZOG' (McCracken and Akscyn, 1984). The underlying principle of the ZOG research was to use simple menu-driven systems in order to make rapid access to large volumes of hypertext and hypermedia material possible.

Two well-known projects that the ZOG group worked on were the data-management system for the nuclear-powered aircraft carrier USS *Carl Vinson* (Kramlich, 1984) and the development of the authoring tool KMS (Knowledge Management System). KMS (Akscyn *et al.*, 1988) is essentially a commercially available version of the authoring environment that was developed in the ZOG project.

Negroponte and the media lab (1976)

As the technical capability of computers, display technology and interaction devices improved, greater interest was shown in multimedia techniques and the development of hypermedia methods for information access. Undoubtedly, some of the most spectacular early developments in these areas were produced by the Architecture Machine Group at the Massachusetts Institute of Technology (MIT) in the late 1970s (Brand, 1988). The MIT group, which included Nicholas Negroponte and Richard Bolt, was heavily involved in the development of visual computer interfaces and techniques for spatial data management (Negroponte, 1981).

Probably one of the most famous of Negroponte's research creations was the 'Dataland' project. In this project the whole room in which the computer user was located (the 'media room') acted as a computer terminal; almost everything in the room was manipulable information. The user could interact and navigate through the information space by means of voice commands, pointing operations and gestures; one important gestural communication technique that was developed at MIT was the 'Put That There' interface (Bolt, 1980). The various types of multimedia information embedded within the system could be presented on wall displays, touch-sensitive TV screens and groups of loud-speakers. Each of the objects displayed in any of the visual displays could be 'zoomed in' on in order to obtain greater detail.

Much of the work at MIT on human–computer interaction (particularly the use of gestures) forms the basis for many other, more sophisticated, interfaces to hypermedia systems. These will be described in more detail later in the discussion of cyberspace and virtual reality systems.

Xerox PARC's NoteCards system (1985)

As interest in hypertext and hypermedia developed so it became important to provide users with appropriate tools to facilitate the creation of non-linear text and hypermedia documents. One of the most well known early authoring tools for hypertext was the NoteCards system developed by Xerox PARC in the USA (Halasz, 1988).

NoteCards is a general hypermedia environment that was developed by Randell Trigg, Thomas Moran and Frank Halasz. As its name suggests, the system embeds a notecard metaphor. That is, the system provides the user with a network of electronic notecards that are interconnected by typed links. Essentially, a notecard is an electronic generalization of a 3″ × 5″ paper notecard. Each card can embed textual or graphical material that can be edited. The network that a user creates using NoteCards serves as a medium in which to represent collections of related ideas. It also provides a structure for organizing, storing and retrieving information. The system includes facilities for displaying, modifying, manipulating and navigating through the information networks that users create.

Peter Brown and GUIDE (1986)

Another early hypertext authoring tool was developed in the mid-1980s by Peter Brown at the University of Kent in the UK (Brown, 1986a; 1986b; Morrall, 1991; Ritchie, 1989). His system was called 'GUIDE' and, although it was developed in an academic environment, it is now marketed by a commercial organization called Office Workstations Limited (OWL). The system can be used on a range of delivery platforms such as IBM PCs, UNIX workstations and Apple Macintosh microcomputers. The original intent of Brown's work was not to produce a hypertext authoring system but 'to develop electronic documents which users would prefer to paper ones' (Ritchie, 1989).

The electronic documents used by GUIDE are composed of a mixture of text (and/or graphics material) and 'buttons'. Buttons are reactive CRT screen areas that a user can select by means of a pointing operation. When a given button is selected, any process that is linked to that button is automatically activated through the linking mechanism that the system supports. Buttons can be of a variety of different types, such as replace-buttons, reference-buttons, glossary-buttons and so on. The button mechanism allows users (whether authors or readers) to expand and contract a document in order to view it at the desired level of detail. GUIDE's use of buttons is in many ways identical to their usage in other hypermedia systems such as NoteCards and HyperCard (see below).

Since taking over responsibility for the further development and promotion of GUIDE, OWL has continued to increase its flexibility by providing a range of different support products and tools such as complex graphics, multiple font selection, a 'guidance' facility and a 'reader' version of the product. GUIDE now allows multimedia connections and the ability to link not only to other documents but also between other applications – a user can, for example, create links between a textual document and a spreadsheet.

Bill Atkinson and HyperCard (1987)

Undoubtedly one of the most popular hypermedia authoring tools in current use is the HyperCard system that was developed originally by Bill Atkinson (Ambron and Hooper, 1990; Goodman, 1987). The HyperCard system is designed to run on Apple Macintosh microcomputer environments. Like the NoteCards system, HyperCard implements a 'notecard' metaphor – that is, CRT screens of information are likened to conventional paper-based index cards in their appearance and function. Some of the main factors influencing the popularity of HyperCard include its ease of use, its extremely low cost and the widespread use of Macintosh computers in many schools and colleges, particularly in the USA.

HyperCard organizes electronic documents into basic units called 'stacks'. Stacks can be interconnected to each other in simple or complex ways to form various types of network structure (see, for example, the structure illustrated in Figure 1.3). Individual stacks are composed from 'cards'. Within a given stack, multimedia cards can be of many different types and can be interlinked in a variety of ways to form either linear or non-linear network structures. Cards usually contain two basic types of information: display material (that is, text or graphics that is to be presented to the user), and control information (in the form of reactive buttons). The appearance of a typical card from a HyperCard stack is illustrated in Figure 1.4.

The card depicted in Figure 1.4 is part of a stack that contains information about the component parts of a bicycle. The diagram shows the card exactly as it would appear on the screen of an Apple Macintosh microcomputer system. Display text is presented on the left-hand side of the screen and a graphic image is presented on the right-hand side. On the very bottom of the screen the reactive

Figure 1.4 *Section of a HyperCard stack*

buttons are represented by a 'house' icon and various kinds of arrow. The left-pointing arrow in the bottom centre of the screen means 'go to the previous card in the stack' (which is displayed if this button is selected). Similarly, the right-pointing arrow means 'go to the next card the stack'. The symbols shown at the bottom of the screen represent 'visible buttons'. As we shall discuss later, cards may also embed any number of 'hidden buttons'.

Shneiderman and Kearsley – Hypertext Hands-On! (1989)

Another very important development which helped to make the use of hypertext and hypermedia more popular was the publication of the textbook *Hypertext Hands-On!* (Shneiderman and Kearsley, 1989). One of the attractive features of this publication was the fact that the text, tables and images contained within the conventional (linear) paper-based book were also provided in electronic form on two 5.25″ magnetic floppy discs. However, the contents of the floppy discs were not arranged in a linear fashion analogous to the paper book, but in a hypertext format. This could be loaded into an IBM PC compatible microcomputer and used instead of (or alongside) the paper-based version. End-user interaction with the information displayed on the computer's CRT screen could be achieved using a conventional keyboard (via the cursor control keys) or by means of a mouse.

The electronic version of *Hypertext Hands-On!* was developed using a hypermedia authoring system called 'HYPERTIES' (Conklin, 1987; Morrall, 1991). HYPERTIES, which was originally called TIES (an acronym for The Interactive Encyclopedia System), was developed by Ben Shneiderman at the Human–Computer Inter-action Laboratory at the University of Maryland in the USA. The system has been used for the development of a wide range of hypermedia applications such as museum exhibits, electronic encyclopaedias, online maintenance manuals and various types of university course. The system is marketed commercially by the Cognetics Corporation in Princeton, New Jersey, USA.

In HYPERTIES the basic units of information that are input to the system are short articles (typically 50 to 1000 words long) which may be interconnected by any number of links. The links are highlighted words or phrases in the article text (see Figure 1.5). Activating a link causes the article about that topic to appear in its own window on the CRT screen. The system keeps track of the user's path through the network of articles thereby enabling easy return from exploratory side paths. In addition to a title and a body of text, each article has a short description (5 to 25 words in length) which the HYPERTIES browser can display very quickly (see, for example, the description of Linz in Figure 1.5). This feature allows the user an intermediate position between calling up the full article associated with a link and trying to guess from the link name precisely what an article is about.

NATO workshop on Hypertext/Hypermedia for Learning (1989)

As interest in the use of hypertext and hypermedia began to become more well established (particularly in educational institu-tions) so many research projects started to develop.

In general, these were intended to identify and solve some of the more important problems relating to the use and application of hypertext and hypermedia techniques. A NATO Advanced Research Workshop, entitled 'Designing Hypertext/Hypermedia for Learning'was held in July 1989 in Rottenburg am Necker in the

Austria (see map) holds a special place in the history of the **Holocaust.**

Situated between Eastern and Western Europe, possessing a vibrant and

culturally creative **Jewish community** on the eve of World War II,

Austria had also provided the young **Adolf Hitler**, himself an Austrian

raised near Linz, with important lessons in the political uses of

antisemitism. Leading **Nazis** came from Austria: the names of Adolf

Hitler, **Adolf Eichmann**, who organized the **deportations** of the Jews to

the **death camps**, and Ernst **Kaltenbrunner**, the head of the

Reich Main Office for Security, 1943-45, readily come to mind.   As

----

Linz - city in northern Austria; childhood home of Adolf Hitler and other

leading Nazis

NEXT PAGE   **RETURN TO GYPSIES**   **INDEX**

Figure 1.5 *Example of a section of hypertext*

Federal Republic of Germany. The workshop brought together over 25 international experts from many of the NATO countries to discuss common problems with respect to learning and training applications of hypermedia.

It was claimed that at the time of the conference there was little evidence that hypertext could successfully support learning outcomes. A limited number of research projects were investigating hypertext for learning, but few conclusions and little if any evidence on how to design hypertext for learning applications were available. The purpose of the workshop was therefore to bring together current users and researchers of hypertext to discuss its current status and potential within educational settings. The NATO workshop was organized to accommodate six basic themes: hypermedia and learning; designing the information model; designing the user interface; hypermedia and instruction; the hypermedia design process; and conceptual foundations for designing hypermedia systems for learning. The workshop included presentations, hardware demonstrations, sharing and browsing of hypertexts and much discussion about each of the above topics. An important outcome of the conference was the production of a book which was intended to capture much of what took place at the workshop (Jonassen and Mandl, 1990). Commenting on the book, the editors wrote in the preface: 'This book is more than a compilation of papers. It is an implementation of the workshop constrained by the limitations of print-on-paper text.'

NATO ASI on Cognitive Tools for Learning (1990)

The NATO workshop described above was just one of many discussions that took place on the educational impact of hypertext and hypermedia during the period 1987 – 1990. Indeed, much interesting debate took place within both Europe and the USA (see, for example, CACM, 1988; McAleese, 1989; McAleese and Green, 1990). One very important theme that emerged from this debate was the idea of incorporating hypermedia techniques into open and distance learning resources, thereby making them more flexible and adaptable. The educational premise behind this approach was that learning environments could be designed which would allow students to 'pick up' just those elements of a subject domain which were missing from their own knowledge and skill repertoire. This idea proved to be very attractive to those educators who could not accommodate the traditions associated with programmed instruction or conventional computer-based training. Beside the potential of navigating through hypermedia resources, educators emphasized the merit of users being able to create their own ideas within a flexible information environment. However, to support this approach to learning, educators realized that many new types of tool would be needed.

In order to bring together researchers who were interested in the development of such tools, Piet Kommer and his colleagues organized a NATO workshop entitled 'Mindtools: Cognitive Technologies for Modelling Knowledge'. This was hosted by the University of Twente at Enschede in The Netherlands during July, 1990. The workshop was organized into six basic themes: semantic networking; expert systems; hypertext; collaborative communication tools; microworlds; and implementing cognitive tools. The proceedings of the workshop were published as an authoritative reference book entitled *Cognitive Tools for Learning* (Kommers *et al.*, 1992). Many of the topics covered in the 1990 NATO conference and its proceedings are further discussed in subsequent sections of this book.

The advent of the multimedia PC (1992)

As well as software developments, the emergence of effective and efficient hypertext/hypermedia systems depended critically upon appropriate developments in hardware technology. Four important breakthroughs were needed: a high-speed, low-cost computational ability; high-resolution display screens to facilitate the presentation of pictures and text; suitable pointing devices (such as the mouse, touch-sensitive screen and tracker-ball); and large-capacity, fast-access storage devices such as those based upon optical disc. By the late 1980s and early 1990s the various types of computer that became commercially available were all able to fulfil all of these requirements. (The technical developments themselves and their relevance to producing hypermedia resources are each explained and discussed in more detail in Chapter 2.)

Despite these developments, the hardware and software available for implementing hypermedia systems still lagged considerably behind the continually expanding requirements of system designers and developers. In his keynote address at the Hypertext '87 conference (CACM, 1988), Andries van Dam remarked:

> If a picture is worth a thousand words, a dynamic picture of time-varying objects is worth a thousand static ones. We need dynamics at the nodes, not just static pictures and text.

The ability to incorporate moving pictures into hypermedia was thus quite a fundamental requirement. Of course, as well as moving pictures, sound resources can also play an important role within a hypermedia system. It is obvious therefore that the complete solution to many of the problems of producing and using hypermedia on a computer depends upon the development of a truly multimedia PC (MPC); that is, one that can support the use of text, static pictures, moving pictures of various sorts, sound – and a variety of different styles of human–computer interaction.

Although the ideal solution to providing a multimedia PC is not yet commercially viable, considerable progress towards meeting this goal is being made. It is anticipated that by the end of the 1990s all microcomputers will have the ability to acquire, store, process and distribute multimedia information. MPCs will have the ability to mix such information in a multitude of different ways and to use those 'media mixes' that are most appropriate to the needs of particular types of hypermedia application. Some of these possibilities will be discussed later in this book.

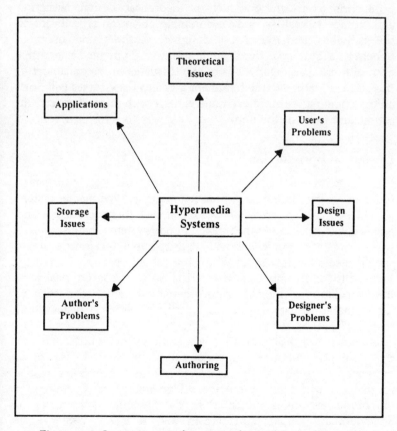

Figure 1.6 *Current issues in designing and using hypermedia systems*

Current activities

Having established some of the important milestones in the development of hypertext and hypermedia, we shall now look at some of the more interesting types of ongoing activity in this area. A useful starting point for an exploration of current activity in hypermedia development and application is the summary diagram shown in Figure 1.6, which is a modified version of one which appears at the beginning of Jonassen's (1989) book on hypertext and hypermedia. Essentially, it expresses current activity in terms of three basic areas of concern. First, approaches to design and production (considerations such as theoretical, design, authoring and storage issues); second, important problem areas (relevant to the activities undertaken by designers, authors and users of hypermedia systems); third, applications of hypermedia systems. Each of these considerations is briefly discussed in the remainder of this section. Naturally, the treatment given to these topics will be of an overview nature since each one is dealt with in greater depth in subsequent parts of the book.

Design and production

Obviously, the design and production of a hypermedia system should be based upon established and well-founded theory and practice with respect to what makes a good system. There are many well-documented guidelines and theories about the form systems should take and the way in which they should behave. Currently, some of the most important theoretical issues of concern deal with the formulation of models and mathematical frameworks (such as formal methods) within which to describe hypermedia systems and their applications.

Design issues deal primarily with those factors which influence the content, structure, appearance and modes of use of a hypermedia system. An important consideration here is the search for the most useful and productive 'design methodology'. A number of approaches are documented in the literature (Martin, 1990; Shneiderman, 1992a; Shneiderman and Kearsley, 1989). One particularly useful methodology that is used by a number of organizations is the 'information mapping' approach, described and advocated by Horn (1989; 1992).

The authoring issues associated with a hypermedia project deal mainly with the processes involved in converting the results of the design phase into either an operational product or a 'prototype' system. For most applications it is unlikely that an operational product will be produced straight off; usually, an experimental prototype is first created. When this has been produced it is tested, evaluated and then revised. Some of the important issues that need to be considered during the authoring process are: 1) choosing a suitable authoring tool(s) and support environment; and 2) selecting appropriate mechanisms for system evaluation. Of course, if the hypermedia system is to be used for pedagogic purposes, then the educational and training objectives must also be identified and realized.

Storage issues within a hypermedia project are concerned with selecting the most appropriate storage medium (in terms of cost, convenience and robustness) upon which to disseminate and deliver the final system. *Hypertext Hands-On!*, for example, is distributed on magnetic disc for installation on and delivery from a computer's hard disc facility (Shneiderman and Kearsley, 1989). Increasingly, digital optical storage media are playing an important role in facilitating the storage, dissemination and delivery of hypermedia systems, particularly in situations where large volumes of text, sound and pictures are involved. We shall discuss the use of optical storage media later in the book.

Problem areas

All of the people involved in designing, creating and using non-linear (hypermedia) information systems will undoubtedly encounter a range of problems that relate to the nature of their individual level of involvement. Fortunately, many of these problems are well-known to hypermedia researchers and so, for most of them, solutions are available.

For designers of hypermedia systems the four most important problems to be overcome are:

1. deciding upon the level and structure of the information to be used for a given application;
2. choosing the most appropriate media mix (text, pictures, sound and so on) to be used;
3. selecting the most suitable modes of end-user interaction with the system; and
4. deciding upon the type of delivery environment (hardware and software) that is to be used for the final product.

Of course, if the system is to be used for learning and training, then mechanisms for checking its educational validity must also be available.

The author of a hypermedia system is the person (or group) who is responsible for creating the operational product from the design documentation. Some of the most difficult problems that this person (or team) has to face will relate to choosing the most appropriate tools for the development tasks; and keeping control of the large volumes of multimedia information that are involved in product development. If these problems are to be handled successfully it is imperative that appropriate development and management tools are employed.

Two of the most important problems faced by users of hypermedia systems relate to navigation and system perception. Navigation is concerned with how users will find their way around the system and locate the particular pieces of information that are of interest to them. As we shall see later, various tools are usually provided to facilitate these tasks. A user's perception of a hypermedia system is related to the way in which that user actually visualizes the system that is being used. This perception will depend upon a variety of factors, such as the nature of the end-user interfaces that are provided and the types of 'metaphor' that are embedded within it. Various types of metaphor (such as electronic books and travel metaphors) are often used to influence a user's perception of a system. The electronic book metaphor is one which we find very useful – it will be discussed in detail later.

Applications

Interest in the use of hypermedia techniques for information storage and delivery has developed substantially in the last few years both in academic and industrial/commercial organizations. Academics see its potential in two basic areas: first, for providing electronic systems for storing and accessing knowledge; second, as a means of developing more flexible approaches to computer-based learning and training. Commercial organizations also appreciate this latter advantage but, in general, see the most useful applications of hypermedia being in the areas of 'product enhancement' and improving organizational efficiency.

Hypermedia organizations of knowledge are particularly well-suited to dictionaries, encyclopaedias, instructional manuals, research handbooks and conference proceedings. Kreitzberg and Shneiderman (1992) also suggest that this approach is useful for producing newsletters, on-line help, instruction and dynamic glossaries, reference manuals, corporate policy manuals, summaries of products and services, employee orientation material, biographies, regulations and procedures, and documenting museum exhibits. We shall discuss some of these types of application later.

Future possibilities

Within any area of endeavour, developments in technology usually affect progress in four important ways. First, technology can be used to extend the limits of what can be done; second, it can affect the speed with which objectives can be realized; third, technology can strongly influence the ease with which activities can be performed; finally, technology can be used to extend an area of endeavour in new directions as a result of providing 'enabling resources'. It is interesting (and the purpose of this section) to speculate on how advances in enabling technologies might influence future developments in hypermedia. Five areas of development will be briefly considered: the impact of new storage media (such as memory cards and digital optical disc); developments in interaction technology; the impact of telecommunications; the implications of artificial intelligence; and the development of new areas and types of application.

The impact of new storage technologies

There are two important aspects of storage technology that are likely to influence developments in the way hypermedia is employed and delivered. First, the availability of high capacity 'credit card' memory systems for PCs; second, the development of compression and decompression techniques for use with both conventional computer storage and digital optical storage media.

Credit card memory systems are growing rapidly in popularity due to their convenience, speed, ease of use and reliability. They are available in several different forms (for example, read-only and re-writable) and in a range of storage capacities. In operation a memory card is a storage device that functions just like a floppy disc. However, since memory cards contain no moving parts they are more robust and more reliable than hard or floppy discs. Memory cards can also be read and written to at much higher speeds than conventional magnetic discs. One common type of memory card is that which conforms to the PCMCIA (Personal Computer Memory Card International Association) standard. Undoubtedly, the availability of this type of storage facility will open up many new application areas for hypermedia, especially in situations where portable PCs and notebook computers are used as delivery platforms.

Increasing use is now being made of facilities for compressing and decompressing material that is stored within computer systems. These techniques are important for two reasons: to increase the amount of information that can be stored; and to increase the speed with which information can be moved from one location to another. Compression and decompression techniques are particularly important for use with digital optical storage media, the most popular form being compact disc read-only-memory (CD-ROM). The storage capacity of a CD-ROM disc is about 650 megabytes — equivalent to about 200,000 pages of A4 typescript or 18 hours of sound (depending on how it is stored). This is quite a substantial amount of storage space for hypermedia applications that deal with textual material, sound and static pictures. However, this medium is unable to store and deliver TV-quality motion pictures unless adequate compression and decompression methods are used. Several techniques are currently available for performing these operations but some degree of standardization will be necessary before CD-ROM will be an effective medium for the delivery of hypermedia material that embeds TV-quality motion pictures.

Developments in interaction technology

Hypermedia is essentially an 'interactive' technology; that is, users point (either directly or indirectly) to reactive objects that are being displayed on a computer screen. These pointing operations enable users to select the particular items of information that are of interest to them. The successful implementation of pointing operations depends upon the availability of a suitable interaction technology, for example, a touch-screen or light pen (for direct pointing) or a mouse, roller controller, joy-stick or tracker-ball (for indirect pointing).

The use of pointing devices similar to those listed above is now well established. However, other types of technology to facilitate pointing operations are being developed. Three of the most interesting of these depend for their success upon the use of a data glove, special goggles/glasses and voice commands. The data glove is a glove-like device that contains embedded position and direction senors that enable a computer to deduce the screen location at which a user is pointing with his or her finger (further details about data gloves are presented in Chapter 6). The use of special purpose goggles or glasses for implementing pointing operations is based upon the use of eye movements and accurate measurements of gaze direction. Using suitable detection equipment it is possible for a computer to deduce the screen location at which a user is looking then, by winking or blinking, a user can action the selection of the particular object that he or she is looking at. Voice driven pointing devices are also likely to become increasingly popular in the future, based upon a limited repertoire of spoken commands such as 'up', 'down', 'left', 'right' and so on.

The impact of telecommunications

There are three basic ways in which telecommunications facilities are likely to influence developments in hypermedia. Essentially, these relate to: 1) the global distribution of hypermedia materials;

2) the provision of shared remote access to resources; and 3) the creation of distributed hypermedia systems. Each of these is briefly discussed below.

Obviously, the availability of a telecommunications network means, in general, that information can easily be moved from one location to another. This implies that such networks can therefore be used to facilitate the dissemination of a hypermedia knowledge corpus to multiple users in a way that is independent of their geographical location. This also means that it now becomes very easy to share hypermedia material, provided the information-carrying capacity of the network (that is, its bandwidth) is sufficient to support the transfer of the embedded multimedia information within a reasonable time-scale.

Alternatively, if the actual dissemination of a hypermedia system is not required, a telecommunications facility can be used to provide distributed access. That is, users who are spread out in different (possibly remote) geographical locations can each simultaneously access (and possibly update) a centrally-located hypermedia knowledge corpus. Obviously, for sensitive information it may be necessary to impose various sorts of access control mechanism that will allow users only to gain access to information for which they have been granted access rights. It may also be necessary to impose charging mechanisms.

As well as facilitating dissemination and distributed access, a telecommunications network can also offer the possibility of implementing a distributed hypermedia system. Such a system is one in which different sections of the overall knowledge corpus are located at different geographical points. The design and implementation of distributed hypermedia systems provide many interesting problems with respect to system update and access; we shall return to a discussion of this type of system in Chapter 6.

The implications of artificial intelligence

Combining artificial intelligence techniques with a hypermedia resource is a natural way of extending and improving the types of facility that can be made available within non-linear information systems. Undoubtedly, one of the most popular ways of proceeding is to combine the capabilities and features of an expert system with those of a hypermedia facility. Rada (1991), for example, has used the term 'expertext' to describe the work he has undertaken in the context of developing 'intelligent hypertext' by augmenting hypertext through the use of expert systems technology. Obviously, in order to undertake developments of this sort it is important to have suitable development tools available. One very useful tool that combines a hypermedia authoring facility and an expert system capability is the KnowledgePro system (Barker, 1989a). This development tool provides a very powerful environment within which to produce a range of different types of intelligent hypermedia system that incorporate appropriate combinations of hypertext, sound and pictures. The development of systems of this type will become much easier as 'integrated systems' and the multimedia PC become more widely available.

As well as using expert system technology within hypermedia applications it is also possible to use other types of tool (such as neural networks) and user-modelling techniques in order to develop flexible and adaptable end-user interfaces to these systems (Hedberg, 1993). By 'building in' a suitable learning facility it is also possible to provide a mechanism that will allow a hypermedia system to adapt its behaviour automatically to meet the communication level, retrieval patterns and information presentation requirements of particular types of user. Developments of this type are likely to have significant impact on the creation of new approaches to the way in which interactive learning and training facilities are provided. One particular example of this is the creation of electronic performance support systems for the provision of just-in-time, on-the-job training (this technique is briefly described in the following section and later in Chapters 4 and 6). Because of the significant potential utility of artificial intelligence some of the different ways of using it within hypermedia will be explored in subsequent sections of this book.

The development of new areas and types of application

As was mentioned in the previous section, the combination of hypermedia with other technologies can be used to extend and enhance the facilities that can be made available. This approach can also be used to produce new types of application. Two important areas of development that are rapidly expanding arise as a result of: 1) combining hypermedia techniques with virtual reality technology in order to produce various types of interlinked 'cyberspace' environment, and 2) integrating expert systems, online retrieval and computer-based training technologies with hypermedia to form a new type of product known as an electronic performance support system (EPSS).

1. Within hypermedia systems we have seen a transition from purely text-based approaches to more sophisticated multimedia applications that incorporate sound, static pictures and moving images. One natural way in which one could extrapolate this trend is towards the use of hypermedia concepts within virtual reality systems (Helsel and Paris Roth, 1991). Virtual reality permits 'total immersion' of a user within an artificial world that is generated by a computer system. In principle, there is no reason why many artificial worlds could not be interlinked through the use of hypermedia techniques. The potential of this approach within training is quite enormous and this possibility is further explored in Chapter 6.

2. An EPSS is an integrated software/hardware system that is designed to deliver on-the-job training and task-orientated job support information within a just-in-time context. That is, an EPSS is a performance support tool (Gery, 1991) for the staff of an organization which is accessed as and when the need arises during the execution of a normal job function. Because of the flexibility that can be obtained from their use, a growing number of EPSS tools are now incorporating hypermedia techniques within the training and support facilities they provide. Examples of the ways in which hypermedia can be used within EPSS facilities will be discussed in greater depth later.

Summary and conclusion

Hypertext and hypermedia concepts have been around for several decades and during this time they have grown substantially in importance. Indeed, nowadays hypermedia techniques are a necessary and important part of an information system designer's repertoire of skills. In this chapter we have presented an outline of the origin of hypermedia and briefly surveyed some of the early developments in this area. Some evidence for the potential utility of this approach to information storage and retrieval has also been presented.

The fundamental principle underlying hypermedia is the concept of making units of screen-based information reactive through the incorporation of either implicit or explicit 'buttons'. These buttons are used to generate links from one unit of information to other related items. Obviously, the linking together of information units is a basic prerequisite for the successful creation of a hypermedia application. The way in which this is achieved is discussed in more detail in Chapter 2.

Within this chapter a number of hypertext/hypermedia 'authoring tools' have been mentioned, such as HyperCard, GUIDE, HYPERTIES and NoteCards. Although these tools were relatively early developments in the history of hypermedia, they are still in wide use today. However, many other tools for the generation of non-linear information systems are now available commercially – such as KnowledgePro, LinkWay and ToolBook. Some of these tools are discussed in Chapter 3.

One of the most important application areas for hypermedia techniques is education and training. As we have suggested earlier in this chapter, there is considerable scope for applying hypermedia concepts to the design of interactive instructional systems in order to improve their flexibility and adaptability from the point of view of potential users. The educational potential of hypermedia is explored in Chapter 4.

Earlier in this chapter we mentioned that 'navigation' in hypermedia systems could be a source of significant problems for users of such systems. Navigation is discussed in more detail in Chapter 2 and subsequently in Chapter 5 where the use of an 'electronic book' metaphor is used to overcome some of the orientation problems that hypermedia users often face.

The basic ideas and concepts underlying the hypermedia approach to information storage and access have not changed in any significant way since Vanevar Bush first put forward his ideas. Although the concepts have not changed, advances in information storage and processing technologies have had, and will continue to have, significant impact on the ways in which these methods and techniques are implemented and used. In the remainder of this book we shall explore some of the possibilities that exist for developing and using hypermedia systems and, in Chapter 6, attempt to identify some potential future directions of development for hypermedia.

2 Technical Perspective

Introduction

Hypermedia is the name given to the collection of technologies and techniques that are needed to create and access non-linear information structures using interactive selection strategies. That is, users select the items of information that they require to see by pointing (either directly or indirectly) to various types of reactive object (such as words or picture elements) that are displayed on a computer screen. Implicit in this approach to information storage and access is the use of a number of basic underlying technologies that together make up the storage system, the computer system, and the human—computer interface system. The relationship between these is illustrated schematically in Figure 2.1.

The storage system is used to store the basic items of multimedia information (text, pictures and sound) that make up the knowledge/ information corpus that underlies a given application. As we shall discuss later, these basic items of information will be interlinked in various ways, the exact nature of the links depending on the purpose for which the information is to be used. The three most commonly used storage technologies for hypermedia are magnetic, electrical and optical.

The computer system is needed in order to provide the necessary hardware and software resources that are required to create the knowledge corpus and subsequently process the information units that it contains. The creation of the knowledge corpus is often referred to as 'authoring' (the authoring process is discussed in greater detail in Chapter 3). The computer system can also be used

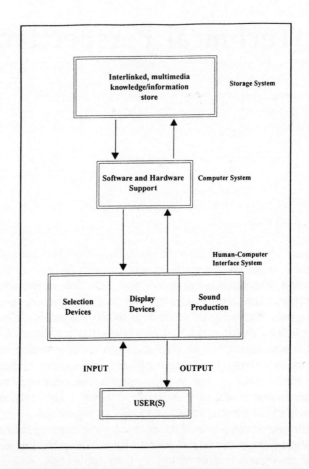

Figure 2.1 *Relationship between the basic components of a hypermedia system*

to provide other functions such as the implementation of security mechanisms (to control access to the knowledge corpus) and the provision of help and guidance facilities (for new users). Each of these features will be discussed in more detail later.

The human–computer interface system performs two basic functions: first, it provides mechanisms to enable users to access, control and update stored information held within the knowledge corpus; and second, it makes available appropriate facilities to enable users to view (and listen to) the items of information that they retrieve. Normally, for the input of information, a keyboard is used for the entry of text while a mouse, touch-screen, trackball or light-pen is used to implement pointing operations (Barker, 1989b). For the output of information, a computer screen is most frequently used (for the display of text and pictures) and audio material is relayed to the user either by means of the computer's internal sound system or an external audio unit.

A basic hypermedia delivery platform

The term 'delivery platform' refers to the basic computer system (and related equipment) that is needed in order to gain access to a hypermedia application. A wide range of possibilities exist, depending upon the type of computer that is used and whether it functions as a stand-alone unit or as part of an interconnected computer network system. One of the simplest types of delivery platform is that based on the use of a 'simple' personal computer (PC) system that is equipped with a CRT screen display, a keyboard and a mouse. A typical PC-based delivery platform is illustrated schematically in Figure 2.2.

The screen will normally be of a high-resolution variety capable of displaying both text and graphics (either individually or in combination). The capacity of the display will be such that, in character mode, it will be capable of displaying up to 25 lines of text each of which can contain up to 80 characters. In graphics mode the screen can be regarded as an array of 1024 (horizontal) by 768 (vertical) multi-coloured picture elements (pixels). The range of colours that the monitor screen is able to display will usually depend upon the type of graphics card that is embedded within the computer. For the display of pictorial information of a reasonable quality it should be able to support a range of at least 256 different colours.

The mouse is connected (either directly or indirectly) to the computer and is used to control the position of an on-screen pointing facility called a cursor. This is denoted by an arrow labelled C in Figure 2.2. As the hand-held mouse is moved around by the user on a flat horizontal surface, its movement is 'echoed' by corresponding movements of the cursor. The mouse has two buttons (labelled B1 and B2 in the diagram) which enable the user to

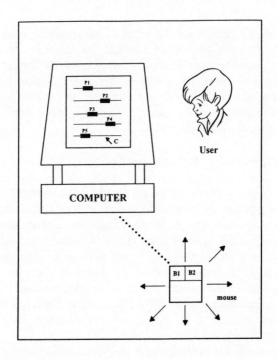

Figure 2.2 *A typical hypermedia delivery platform*

send simple signals to the computer. By pressing one or other of the buttons the user is able to indicate to the computer that the item currently 'under the cursor' is the one that is required. This approach to using a mouse to select items is commonly referred to as the 'point and click' method. Notice that although the functionality of the two mouse buttons is usually the same, in some applications they can serve different purposes.

The screen depicted in Figure 2.2 is meant to be displaying some lines of hypertext. Within these lines of text certain words and phrases (labelled P1 to P5) have been designated to be reactive 'buttons'. That is, when one of them is selected by moving the cursor to it and then clicking a mouse button, another process associated with the selected item is initiated, usually resulting in the production of sound or the presentation of further text (or pictures) on the CRT screen. For example, if each of the items P1 to P5 represented the name of an animal, then clicking on a button might generate a sound effect or initiate the display of a picture of the animal whose name was selected.

Where next?

So far in this chapter we have discussed the essential principles underlying the delivery of hypermedia information – the nature of the delivery platform and how it is used. In subsequent sections we shall explore the types of underlying information structure that are needed to support hypermedia applications, the nature of interactive buttons, the basic principles underlying the creation of hypertext and hypermedia (authoring), navigation problems and support tools to enable people to create and use hypermedia systems.

Non-linear information structures

Information (and knowledge) can be organized in a variety of different ways. Naturally, the way in which these commodities are organized and stored can significantly influence their meaning and the purposes for which they can be used. Two basic approaches are often used for organizing (and presenting) information and knowledge, often referred to as the linear and the non-linear approaches. A graphical comparison of these two different methods of organization is presented in Figure 2.3. Each approach is further discussed below.

Linear structures

The essential idea underlying a linear organization is that a corpus of knowledge is organized into several units (A, B, C, D and E in Figure 2.3) which are designed to follow each other in sequence, although some jumping back or skipping ahead is usually allowed. As can be seen from Figure 2.3, each of the basic units from which a linear structure is composed has just one entry point and one exit. Another important point to note (see Figure 2.4a) is that the material embedded within each module that makes up a linear

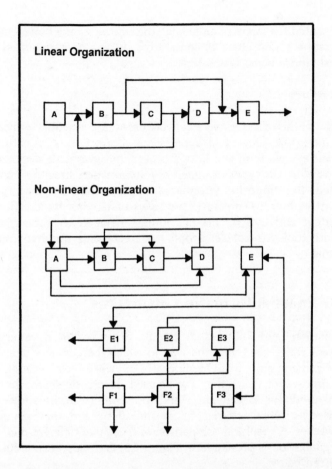

Figure 2.3 *Linear and non-linear arrangements of knowledge*

information structure is intended to be processed in a strictly sequential fashion.

The linear approach has, until recently, been one of the most widely used types of organizational structure. Indeed, it forms the basis of many of the most commonly used methods of organizing and presenting knowledge. Consider, for example, the collection of chapters from which this book is composed – they are arranged into a particular sequence in order to achieve a certain effect. Each chapter is composed of a number of sections each of which is made up from a series of paragraphs. Paragraphs are composed of sentences which, in turn, are built from sequences of words. Although readers may not choose to access the book in this fashion, it is certainly the way in which the author intended it to be used – at least on first reading!

Sentences are examples of a strictly 'linear' arrangement of information. Each word in a sentence occupies a particular position and sentences are constructed in such a way that a reader commences at the first word in a sentence and processes each subsequent word in turn until a full stop is encountered. A similar strategy applies to the processing of paragraphs; the first sentence in a paragraph is processed, then the second, then the third and so on, until the end of the paragraph is reached. Sections and chapters are also essentially linear in their basic design and structure. So too are the majority of conventional books that are published on paper – it would not be very meaningful to read the pages of a 'detective story' in any order other than the sequential one specified by its author – unless the reader wishes to skim or scan the text. Conventional books thus provide a good example of an essentially linear information storage and presentation mechanism.

Many other types of media also impose a linear structure onto the information they store. Two common examples are audio tape and film. Each of these storage media is intended to store information units (and subsequently present them) in a strictly sequential fashion. A tape-slide presentation is another good example of a linear presentation method for information.

Non-linear structures

Some information storage and presentation media (particularly those which embed some form of computer facility) allow significant departures from the basic linear strategies described above. The essential features of a non-linear approach are illustrated in the lower part of Figure 2.3. In this diagram the basic units of information (A, B, C, etc.) that make up the knowledge corpus are joined together in many complex ways that allow them to be processed in a variety of different non-linear pathways. This is made possible because each of the modules used in this type of arrangement has one entry point but can have any number of exit points (see Figure 2.4b). Therefore, from within the body of one unit it is possible for the user to 'jump' to any of a number of other units depending upon his or her information interests and requirements. Thus, from unit A (in Figure 2.3) the user can proceed to unit B, C, D or E; then, from unit E it is possible to proceed to unit A or to unit E1. Similarly, from unit E1 the user can go to unit E3 or to some other related point in the knowledge corpus.

As can be seen from Figure 2.4, the essential feature of a non-linear information/knowledge unit is the existence of embedded 'decision points' at which the user has to make a decision about which way to proceed. For example, at Decision Point 1, the user can choose to exit (through Exit 1) or carry on within the same unit; at Decision Point 2 a similar choice is available – carry on or leave the unit via Exit 2. Similarly, at Decision Point 3 the user can choose to leave the unit via any of three different routes (Exits 3, 4 or 5).

Each of the exits from an information unit will usually lead to a different outcome. Also, when a given exit is chosen the user may leave the current 'host' information unit permanently, temporarily or transiently, depending upon the effects that the hypermedia designer wants to achieve. Each of these possibilities will be discussed in more detail later.

The decision-making inherent in using a non-linear information structure is performed interactively by the user. Usually, decisions are made using the 'point and click' facility provided by the pointing device that is attached to the delivery platform being used to present a hypermedia application. An important aspect of hypermedia design is the way in which users are made aware of the decision points that are embedded within information units. This topic is discussed in the following section.

Reactivity – buttons and links

As we discussed in the previous section, the successful use of hypermedia technology depends critically upon the design and creation of suitable non-linear information structures that are appropriate to the interactive application being produced. These information structures must be designed in such a way that they

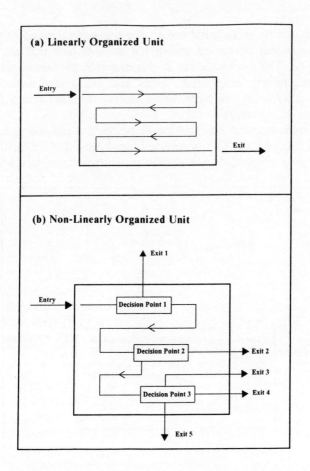

Figure 2.4 *Linear and non-linear information/knowledge units*

embed decision points that allow users to choose the 'direction' in which they wish to proceed through the underlying knowledge corpus associated with a given application. This requirement is usually accomplished by embedding 'reactive areas' within the screen-based information that is displayed to users.

As an example, consider the section of hypertext depicted schematically in Figure 2.5. This shows how a piece of textual material can embed seven reactive areas. In this diagram these areas are denoted by rectangular boxes that are drawn around certain of the key words contained within the lines of text that are being displayed. The reactive areas in this example are the words 'cats', 'mother', 'father', 'dogs', 'fish', 'birds' and 'chickens'. Reactive areas within a hypertext or hypermedia screen are often referred to as 'buttons' or 'hotspots'.

A reactive screen area (button or hotspot) is defined as being a special area of the CRT screen which can be selected by the user by means of a point and click operation. Each reactive area within a

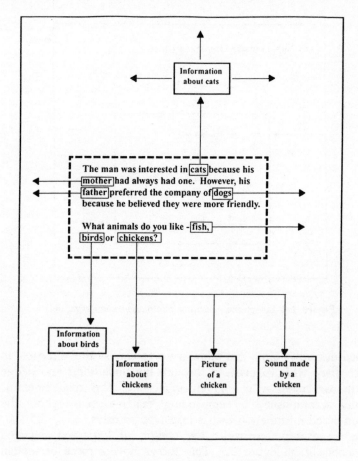

Figure 2.5 *Reactive areas within a section of hypertext*

given screen display will usually be associated with (or 'linked' to) a number of other objects, processes or activities that will be invoked when their parent hotspot is selected. Thus, in Figure 2.5, the 'cats' hotspot is linked to another information unit which gives further information about cats. Similarly, the 'dogs' hotspot is linked to an information unit that gives more information about dogs. Because each of the information units associated with the hotspots in Figure 2.5 will themselves also have embedded hotspots and links it is possible for a user to embark on an 'exploratory journey' through the associated knowledge corpus. Because the journey will be non-linear it will usually be difficult to predicate beforehand where a user will ultimately end up.

The reactive areas within a piece of hypertext are not normally indicated by actually drawing rectangles around words or phrases as has been done in Figure 2.5 – this approach would be difficult, tedious and time-consuming. Some alternative mechanism therefore has to be used. Usually, reactive words or phrases within a text corpus are denoted by making them a different colour from the words that make up the unreactive text. For example, the designer of a particular hypertext application might decide to use the following colour combinations for the screen display of text: blue for background; white for normal unreactive text and yellow (or red) for reactive text. Of course, different colours (or effects such as bold or italics) could be used to denote different kinds of hyperlink, such as a link to another information unit, a glossary definition or a pronunciation.

Suppose that in the example shown in Figure 2.5 we had used the colour yellow to denote reactive text. Readers of this screen could now instantly see where the available decision points are. Thus, if a reader is particularly interested in dogs the cursor could be moved to this word and a mouse button clicked. This would then cause further information on dogs to be displayed which, in turn, might allow a story-line about dogs to unfold. Similarly, if the user moves the mouse cursor to the word 'chickens' this might initiate the display of a multimedia story about chickens – and so on.

In a hypermedia system a combination of different media types (text, sound and pictures) is often used. However, just as it is easy to make text reactive, so in a similar fashion parts of pictures can also be made reactive. It is also possible to embed reactivity within other graphical screen-based objects such as special-purpose buttons and 'icons'. Icons are small graphical objects that provide access to various kinds of system control function or special kinds of tool that are needed by particular applications. Some examples of icons can be seen on the HyperCard screen illustrated in Figure 1.4. In this illustration there are four icons – a small house and three different types of arrow. The house icon (in the bottom left-hand corner) is called the 'home button' because selecting it always returns the user to the starting point of the application. The three arrows, which lie to the right of the house, are examples of 'navigation' buttons and allow the user to move explicitly from one information unit to another – navigation is explained later in this chapter.

From what has been said in this section it is easy to see that, along with the basic information units, buttons and links are the essential items needed to build non-linear information structures. The overall process of building these structures involves three important steps:

- the reactive buttons within a given information unit must be identified and made visible to users;
- the target information units that are associated with each of the buttons must be identified (and created if they do not already exist);
- each of the identified buttons must be linked to its associated target information units.

The way in which the interlinking operations are carried out will be described in more detail in the following section. As we shall explain later, special types of software tool (called 'authoring systems') are available to facilitate the building of hypertext and hypermedia applications.

Creating hypertext and hypermedia

When designing and producing hypermedia applications it is useful to have available an appropriate 'development model' that can be used to specify and interrelate the various steps and processes that are involved. Such a model is illustrated schematically in Figure 2.6. One fairly obvious limitation of this model is its linear nature.

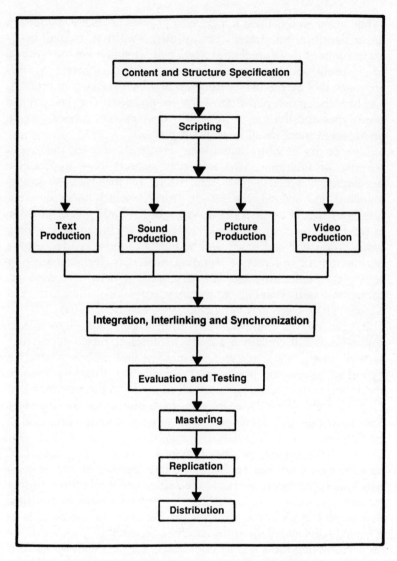

Figure 2.6 *Basic hypermedia development model*

While many well-defined hypermedia projects are likely to follow a linear development strategy, many others will not. Indeed, many more complex development projects will often involve the creation of a 'prototype' system (Philips IMS, 1992). Inherent in this approach will be the use of iteration and back-tracking in order to identify the most beneficial way to proceed. The creation of prototypes and the use of non-linear development models will be discussed in more detail later in Chapter 3.

Despite its obvious limitations, Figure 2.6 serves the useful purpose of indicating two important aspects of a hypermedia development project: first, the nature of the basic processes involved and second, the rough order in which these different processes should be performed. Many of the basic processes listed in the figure, such as content and structure specification, scripting, video production and so on, will be similar to those involved in the production of interactive training materials for delivery by computer. These processes are described in detail in books on computer-based training and interactive video (Bergman and Moore, 1990; Dean and Whitlock, 1992; Harrison, 1991).

In general, as can be seen from Figure 2.6, hypermedia applications will contain a variety of different media types such as text, sound, static pictures, animations and motion video. An important aspect of hypermedia design will therefore involve specifying which media types are to be used and the functions that they will fulfil. Once these decisions have been made the necessary resources can be developed and integrated into the overall application.

As we discussed in the previous section, one important consideration that has to be taken into account is the way in which different media elements are subsequently interlinked (using buttons and their associated links) in order to produce the final hypermedia application. Obviously, the way in which this is achieved will depend upon the nature of the authoring tools that are used. Authoring tools will be discussed in greater depth later in this chapter and in Chapter 3; in this section we consider only the basic principles that are involved in interlinking media elements together. In the discussion that follows we consider (for the purpose of illustration) the use of only two different media element types: text and static pictures.

The interlinking process referred to above (and in Figure 2.6) requires that a reactive area in one media element (called the source element) is linked to at least one other media element (called the target). As can be seen from Figure 2.7, this linking is achieved through the use of buttons which may be of any shape and size. So, the two questions that now arise are: 1) How are the buttons created? and 2) How are they linked to their target media elements?

The way in which buttons are created will depend upon the basic nature of the media element that contains them. When a media element is composed of text then the buttons will usually consist of words or phrases (see Figure 2.5). The special sections of text that make up the reactive buttons can be specified during the authoring process in two basic ways – either interactively or by embedding special control codes within the corpus of text that makes up the media element. The interactive approach usually involves using a mouse to drag a suitably shaped cursor (such as an I-beam) over the words that are to make up a reactive button. The other approach, based on embedded control codes, involves placing a special marker (such as #m ... #m or < < ... > >) around the word sequence that makes up a button. The use of embedded codes within a text corpus forms the basis of the use of special 'mark-up languages' such as SGML for the creation of hypertext (Woodhead, 1991; Wright, 1992).

The markers that are embedded in a text corpus are not displayed to a user who views the hypertext. The markers are simply used by the hypertext delivery system to mark the text buttons in an appropriate colour or font. Once the buttons have been specified the names of the target media elements to which they are linked must be specified. This is done using a 'link table'. An example of a marked section of a hypertext corpus and its associated link table is illustrated in the lower part of Figure 2.7.

Pictorial media elements are usually marked interactively. Again, two approaches are commonly used, based on the use of points or rectangular shaped buttons. In both cases a point and click dialogue is used. In the case of buttons that are points (or small circles) the author of the pictorial media element uses the mouse to position the screen cursor at the location where a button is to be created; a click operation then causes the button to be placed on the picture beneath the cursor. Similarly, in the case of rectangular buttons,

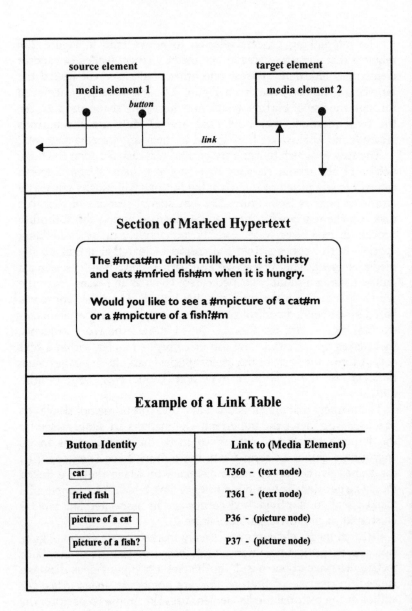

Figure 2.7 *Creating hypertext and hypermedia*

multiple point and click operations can be used to define the reactive area or, alternatively, a special 'marking tool' (in the form of a resizable, relocatable, rectangular shaped cursor) can be employed. As in the case of textual media elements, once a picture has been marked with buttons, a link table has to be created in order to specify which other media elements must be invoked when a given button is selected.

Depending upon how a hypermedia application is designed, the position of reactive buttons in a picture (or in text for that matter) can be hidden, implicit or revealed. Revealed buttons are obviously directly visible to the user. Implicit buttons will be apparent to the user from the context in which they are used. Hidden buttons are not directly visible to the user and are only displayed as the user 'explores' the interface; they can, however, usually be temporarily revealed by means of some form of help facility.

Navigation

As we have previously illustrated, both in Figure 1.3 and in Figure 2.3, the objects within a hypermedia knowledge corpus can be interlinked in many different ways, depending on the needs of the particular application(s) it is intended to serve. Because of the virtually unlimited number of ways in which the multimedia elements of a knowledge corpus can be joined together, it is possible to create extremely complex hypertext and hypermedia structures. The complexity of these structures is illustrated schematically in Figure 2.8 which shows a typical 'net-like' hypermedia web structure.

A user of the knowledge corpus shown in Figure 2.8 may wish to start exploring the structure of the system at the point (or node) labelled A. That user may then wish to proceed from this point to other nodes in the structure and eventually exit from the system at another point, such as the node labelled Z. In order to accomplish this task the hypermedia network must be traversed by moving from one node to another using the links that the system provides. As we saw earlier, as a user encounters a node (such as that shown in Figure 2.4,b or the one presented in Figure 2.5) a series of decisions has to be made about which way to go. It is therefore

EXIT

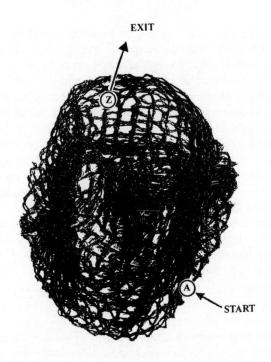

START

Figure 2.8 *Web structure depiction of a hypermedia knowledge corpus*

important to consider how a user might make the navigational decisions that are needed in order to go from one point in a hypermedia structure to another.

Any of a number of different types of decision strategy could be used to explore a hypermedia structure. Three of the most common approaches are: 'trial and error'; use of a 'guided tour'; and by using various sorts of navigation tool.

The trial and error approach to navigation simply involves 'jumping' from one node in a hypermedia structure to another in a more or less random way, that is, without having any underlying rationale which governs the decision about which node to proceed to. Sometimes, this approach to accessing a knowledge corpus is referred to as 'browsing'. Obviously, using this type of approach can often lead to 'getting lost', that is, arriving at a point in a structure which has no meaning whatsoever for the user. Getting lost also implies that the user is in a situation in which he or she does not know what to do in order to get to a position of familiarity.

An alternative way of proceeding through a knowledge corpus is by means of a 'guided tour'. A guided tour is simply a sequence of nodes that have been selected on behalf of a user by the designer of the hypermedia system. When on a guided tour, a user is allowed to undertake a limited amount of 'controlled' exploration. However, because of the way a guided tour is designed, users cannot normally get lost. Usually the designer of a hypermedia system will provide a range of guided tours from which a user can select any of those that are appropriate. Guided tours may be organized on either a thematic or a functional basis.

Many users of a hypermedia system will not wish to use guided tours and so will want to explore a structure on their own, making rational rather than random decisions about where they are going. To facilitate this approach, it is important to provide various types of navigation aid which will help the user to make logical decisions about where to go next in the corpus in order to achieve some particular objective. One of the most commonly used navigational aids within hypermedia applications is the 'concept map'.

Concept maps are normally used to provide users with an indication of the type of material that is held in a knowledge corpus. Such maps can also be used to facilitate navigation. An example of the way in which a concept map can be used is illustrated in Figure 2.9 which shows two cards from the HyperCard help system (Goodman, 1987).

Each of the ten 'tabs' at the bottom of the screen represents a hotspot. A hotspot can be selected and activated by moving the cursor (a small hand) over its tab and then clicking a mouse button. Clicking on the 'Map' tab shown in the upper part of the diagram causes the map shown in the lower part of the figure to appear on the screen. This map shows the relationship between and organization of the different items of information held in the help system. Notice how the map indicates the user's current location in the corpus. In order to use the map to get to any particular part of the system the user simply has to move the cursor to the node of interest and then click a mouse button.

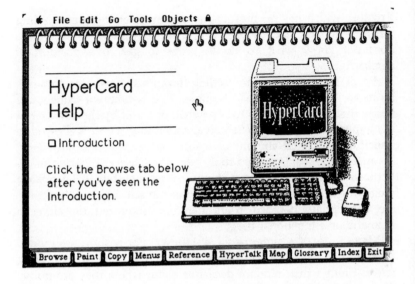

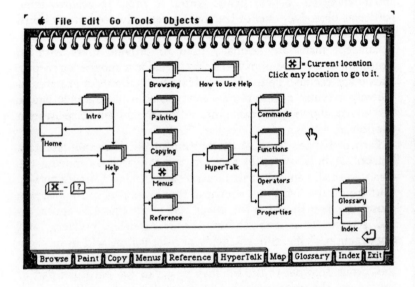

Figure 2.9 *Use of a map for navigation in HyperCard*

Of course, even when navigation aids are provided, users can still get lost unless suitable steps are taken to minimize the chance of this happening. This is usually achieved through the provision of additional tools and mechanisms such as 'signposts', 'anchor points', 'back-tracking' tools and help facilities. Each of these facilities is normally provided by means of appropriately designed sets of reactive buttons.

Signposts are mechanisms which 'point' the user in a particular direction; clicking on a signpost button will move the user towards a particular pre-defined goal. Anchor points are fixed, well-defined locations within the knowledge corpus that the user is likely to be familiar with and which can easily be reached if and when the need arises; the main system menu for an application is often used as an anchor point (the 'Home Card' in the HyperCard system is a good example of this). Back-tracking is a mechanism that allows the user to retrace his or her steps so as to go back to a previously visited part of the hypermedia corpus. Help facilities can take a variety of different forms, such as the provision of a contents list, an index or a set of instructions giving details about how to recover from a difficult situation.

As well as explicit navigational tools similar to those described above it is also possible to provide aids to navigation through the use of appropriately designed metaphors. Usually, these serve to superimpose an 'already familiar' conceptual structure over the knowledge corpus. The aim of this is to make the hypermedia system more understandable to users. Typical metaphors that are currently commonly used in hypertext systems include 'point and question', 'electronic books', 'talking books' and so on. The use of a book metaphor as a navigational aid is described in more detail in Chapter 5.

Support tools

The support tools needed for the development and use of a hypermedia system fall into three broad categories. First, those that are needed to support the authoring processes involved in creating and maintaining a hypermedia knowledge corpus – as we have already established, these are often referred to as authoring tools.

Second, those that are needed to facilitate navigation through the corpus and the subsequent control of information retrieval and display — we shall refer to these as navigation and access tools. Third, there are usually various collections of ancillary tools that may be needed in order to use the system or perform various tasks related to the underlying application that the hypermedia system implements. Each of these different categories of tool is briefly described in this section.

Authoring tools

As we mentioned earlier in this chapter, the process of creating a hypertext or hypermedia system is usually undertaken using a suitable authoring system such as GUIDE, HyperCard, HYPERTIES, ToolBook and so on. Some of these authoring environments have already been briefly described in Chapter 1. Some of the others will be discussed in more detail in the following chapter.

The 'power' of an authoring environment will depend upon the quality and range of tools that it makes available. Usually, as a basic minimum, an authoring environment should provide tools for:

1. creating multimedia information units;
2. marking reactive areas within these units;
3. linking reactive areas within one source unit to appropriate target units in order to create a network structure;
4. importing both marked (using a mark-up language) and unmarked information units for incorporation into the hypermedia network that is being built;
5. updating the network after it becomes operational; and
6. controlling the 'access rights' of the users of the hypermedia corpus (that is, controlling who can do what with respect to viewing, changing and deleting stored information).

The control of access rights (item 6) is imperative since it is extremely important to ensure that the accuracy and integrity of the information held in a knowledge corpus is maintained at all times. Based upon access rights a variety of different types of user can be identified: those who are allowed to read subsets of the stored information; those allowed to read all information; those who can read and update (but not delete) stored information; and those who have full access rights. Of course, access to a hypermedia system may have to be controlled on the basis of whether or not a user belongs to a particular 'stereotype'. Thus, in a training system, unless a user satisfies certain prerequisite skill requirements, he or she may be barred from using certain pathways through a knowledge corpus. (Educational access to hypermedia systems is further discussed in Chapter 4.)

Two other important classes of tool that it is important to include in an authoring environment are testing tools and productivity tools. Testing tools provide the mechanism by which a hypermedia author can test a product and check that it functions correctly before it is replicated and distributed to users (see Figure 2.6). As their name suggests, productivity tools are used in order to increase the productivity of a hypermedia author by automating some of the processes that are involved in creating a knowledge corpus. A range of testing and productivity tools now exists and some of them will be discussed in detail later.

Navigation and access tools

Within a hypermedia system one of the most important types of navigation tool is the concept map; the way in which such maps are used has already been explained in the previous section. A range of other types of diagrammatic form can also be used to indicate a user's location and the alternatives that are available at any particular decision point within a hypermedia corpus. The types of diagrammatic form that are used (pictures, floor plans, street plans, atlas entries and so on) will obviously depend upon the application to be supported. For example, 'Glasgow Online' (a hypermedia corpus designed to provide information about the city of Glasgow) makes extensive use of street plans (Baird, 1990). In a similar way, 'Compton's Multimedia Encyclopedia' makes extensive use of a screen-based atlas in order to facilitate navigation to sources of information about countries of interest (Britannica Software, 1990; 1991).

Two other important types of navigation tool that are often used in a hypermedia system are 'finders' and 'browsers'. A finder is a software tool that is used to locate a particular information unit based upon a user's specification of its required attributes or properties – the properties that can be used will depend upon the way in which a given system has been specified and built. A browser is also a software tool; this type of tool allows a user to move randomly (or otherwise) from one location in a hypermedia network to another, usually based upon a knowledge of the identity of the nodes to be visited.

As well as navigation tools, many other types of facility can be used to help users locate and access the items of information they require. We have already mentioned content lists and indexes. Another type of facility that is often found useful (particularly for textual information units) is full-text retrieval. This technique allows hypermedia nodes containing a given combination of words or phrases to be located. The use of this approach will be described in greater detail later.

Ancillary tools

A hypertext or hypermedia corpus will usually have been designed and fabricated in order to meet some particular application requirement. A range of ancillary support tools will therefore be required in order to enable users to perform particular tasks and achieve specified goals, as dictated by the nature of the underlying application domain. Ancillary support tools are normally classified according to two basic properties: specificity and globality. Each of these properties is briefly discussed below.

Generic and application orientated tools
In terms of their specificity, ancillary support tools may be classified into two basic categories: generic tools and application-specific tools. Generic tools are essentially independent of the underlying application. Three examples of this class of tool are 'notebook', 'annotation' and 'bookmark' tools. The first of these enables users to copy pieces of information from a hypermedia corpus and 'paste' them into personal electronic notebooks for future reference or for subsequent printing (if a generic print tool is not available). An annotation tool allows users to attach personal annotations to a hypermedia node, either for personal use or for sharing with others. A bookmark tool allows users to place their own 'markers' against those hypermedia nodes that are of particular interest to them and to which they may wish to return later.

Application orientated tools are ones that are designed and developed (or tailored) specifically for the underlying application. For example, a hypermedia system for teaching mathematics might require its users to have access to an electronic screen-based calculator, a spread-sheet and a library of mathematical functions. Similarly, a hypermedia package for teaching foreign languages might require language dictionaries (in electronic form) to facilitate translation exercises and audio dictionaries (to show how words and phrases are pronounced).

Of course, as was suggested above, some tools which may be essentially generic in nature may need to be tailored to meet the specific needs of the underlying application. This is particularly the case with glossaries and help systems.

Local and global tools

The range over which a given tool (or set of tools) operates is another important consideration. Some tools will function at all points throughout a hypermedia system; these are called global tools. Usually, glossaries, dictionaries, help systems, notepads, annotation tools and bookmarkers will function in a global fashion. Alternatively, many types of tool will often only function in particular sections of the hypermedia system or in very special well-defined contexts; these are referred to as local tools.

Examples of global and local tools can be found in many hypermedia products such as 'Compton's Multimedia Encyclopedia' (Britannica Software, 1990; 1991) and Elsevier's 'Active Library on Corrosion' (Bogaerts and Agema, 1992). 'Compton's Multimedia Encyclopedia', for instance, makes different toolsets available depending upon what a user happens to be doing. Thus, a standard English dictionary (a global tool) is available at all times in order to enable users to look up the meaning of words that they do not understand. In contrast, the 'compass' and 'grid' tools (both of which have only local scope) only become accessible when someone is using the atlas facility and requires to navigate the globe or manipulate latitude and longitude lines on a map, respectively.

Obviously, when designing tools and toolsets for use in hypermedia applications it is important to give considerable thought to the mode (local or global) in which they should operate. This is particularly true in the case of educational hypermedia systems where there is significant potential for the provision of ancillary support tools.

Conclusion

Hypertext and hypermedia provide extremely powerful mechanisms for the creation of flexible and adaptable information storage and retrieval systems based upon the use of non-linear information structures. As we shall see in a later chapter, such structures, if used carefully, can be used to generate highly stimulating and motivating computer-based interactive learning and training systems.

The delivery of hypermedia resources within such interactive learning environments depends critically upon two important factors: first, the quality of the end-user interfaces that are provided (including toolsets); and second, the supporting information display technologies that are embedded within the delivery platform that is used to present information to users. In this chapter we have established that 'pointing operations' (using a mouse, for example) form an important part of the end-user interface to a hypermedia system. Similarly, we have also emphasized the necessity of using high-resolution colour screens that are capable of displaying text, high quality pictures and motion video. Of course, the use of sound facilities must also be catered for, particularly in situations where hypermedia techniques are being used for language learning (Ingraham and Emery, 1991).

The facile creation of hypermedia resources (through button creation and linking) is a fundamental requirement of potential users of the hypermedia approach to information handling – this is especially true if it is to become widely used for education and training purposes. The availability of suitable authoring tools and publication media (such as magnetic disc and optical disc) must therefore be considered.

In the following chapter we shall turn our attention to some of these issues. We shall take a closer look at authoring environments, design considerations and 'object orientation'. We shall also explore the different publication technologies that are available for storing and delivering hypermedia resources.

3 Tools and Techniques

Introduction

In the previous two chapters of this book we have considered the various background topics that are needed to facilitate an understanding of hypermedia techniques. In subsequent chapters (4, 5 and 6) we shall turn our attention to the ways in which hypermedia methods can be used to promote learning and training activities through the use of purpose-built hypermedia packages, electronic books and various consumer products, such as 'Compton's Multimedia Encyclopedia' and Elsevier's Active Library series (both of which are examples of hypermedia publications). The purpose of the present chapter is to consider some of the practical issues relating to the design and production of hypermedia materials for use in instructional contexts.

The tools, techniques, design and development methods that a particular individual, group or organization will adopt in order to create hypermedia resources will vary considerably from one situation to another. Decisions relating to choices of design approach, development strategy and delivery environment will be influenced by many different factors – budget, installed equipment base, institutional policy and so on. In addition to the normal financial and time constraints that usually accompany a conventional educational development project there will be many other issues to consider when hypermedia techniques are also involved.

From a design and development perspective four of the most important factors that have to be taken into account when producing a hypermedia system are:

- the characteristics of the target audience for which the resources are intended;
- the nature of the underlying design paradigm that is to be employed;
- the type of authoring environment that will be used for producing hypermedia material; and
- the type of delivery platform through which this material will be presented.

Each of these issues is addressed in this chapter.

As would be the case with any other software product, when designing a hypermedia system it is important to consider the nature and characteristics of the target audience that will eventually use it. Some important factors that should therefore be considered are: the type of end-user interface that is required; the type and level of material that will be embedded in the underlying knowledge corpus; and the style of presentation that individual users might prefer. Each of these topics will raise a number of important design considerations, some of which are discussed below.

Before active design of a hypermedia system commences it is important to decide upon an appropriate design and development methodology. One very useful paradigm that is becoming increasingly popular (both for design and implementation) is known as the 'object oriented' approach (Barker, 1992a; Winblad *et al.*, 1990). This method regards a hypermedia system as being built from a collection of reactive objects, each of which can 'communicate' with the other by message passing. Within such a system, whenever an object receives a suitable activation message it reacts in an appropriate manner, usually by sending more messages to other software and hardware objects that are embedded within the system. Because of its importance, object orientation is discussed in more detail below.

At some stage during a hypermedia project a major decision that has to be made is the choice of authoring environment. Ideally, decisions about the authoring tools that are to be used will not normally be made until after the specification and basic design stages of a project are complete. The individual characteristics of specific authoring tools should therefore have had only a relatively minor influence on the design process. As we have suggested in the previous chapter, the function of an authoring facility is twofold: to provide a set of tools to facilitate product development; and to provide a run-time environment to enable users to access the information embedded within that product. The major impact of an authoring environment will therefore normally be felt during the development phase of a project and subsequently, during product use. A wide range of authoring environments is currently available. Some representative examples are described and discussed in this chapter.

The nature of the delivery platform that is used to deliver a hypermedia product is another factor which will also have a significant influence on the way in which a product is designed. Undoubtedly, the most common delivery platform will be some form of personal computer that is fitted with a high-resolution screen and a pointing device (as described in Chapter 2). Naturally, the nature of the PC can vary quite enormously; for example, it may be a desktop system, a portable PC, a notebook computer, a hand-held facility or a consumer product such as CDTV or CD-I (these are discussed later in the book). Each of these delivery platforms will provide different facilities and capabilities (such as screen sizes, interaction devices and storage peripherals) which hypermedia designers need to be aware of. Obviously, the storage devices that are attached to a delivery station will strongly influence how a hypermedia system is accessed and delivered. Increasingly, digital optical storage devices are being used within hypermedia delivery stations, making available substantial volumes of material due to their large storage capacity. Because of their importance we shall return to a discussion of storage devices later.

Bearing in mind the introductory comments that have been made in this section, the basic rationale for the remainder of this chapter is as follows. First, we shall explore some hypermedia design issues; then we will discuss object orientation and authoring tools; and finally, we shall review the various storage media that are available for the delivery of hypermedia resources.

Design considerations

The production of a successful hypermedia product depends critically upon the adoption of a sound and systematic design strategy that is based upon the use of well-founded guidelines and established design procedures, where these exist. Fortunately, there is a wealth of literature available which documents many useful ideas and approaches; see, for example, Begoray (1990), Horn (1989), Kreitzberg and Shneiderman (1992), Martin (1990), Shneiderman (1992a) and Shneiderman and Kearsley (1989).

This section of the book examines some of the more important design issues that need to be considered during a hypermedia project. Three aspects of design are discussed: basic principles, end-user interfaces, and the use of prototypes.

Basic principles

The starting point for the design of a hypermedia system will obviously depend upon the nature of the particular project involved. Fortunately, most projects fall into one or other of two broad categories: designing from 'scratch'; and converting and/or restructuring an existing operational system into a hypermedia format. In this section we shall be primarily concerned with the first of these two approaches. Naturally, much of what is said will also apply to other projects which involve conversion or restructuring.

In what follows we shall assume that a need for a new hypermedia product (for use within a particular application domain) has been identified. We must therefore consider the nature of the subsequent design processes that must be completed in order to produce the final product.

Top-level application design
Before detailed design can commence it is important to resolve a number of 'top-level' design decisions relating to the overall application design; these decisions will significantly influence the way in which subsequent stages of the design will unfold. Some of the important decisions that have to be made will relate to answering the following basic questions:

- What are the aims of the product?
- How will the product be accessed by the user?
- What will the final 'package' consist of?
- What type(s) of user is the product aimed at?

- What form of access control will be needed?
- How will users understand the product?

As we have suggested earlier, the characteristics of the delivery platform (such as pointing mechanism, storage medium, display device and so on) will dictate how the user accesses the product. This decision will therefore also influence certain aspects of design — mainly, the nature of the end-user interface that is produced.

Because the final hypermedia package will usually consist of more than just interactive computer software, it is important to decide what other supporting materials will need to be supplied and what format they should take. In many situations a user-guide will be needed. Sometimes one or more workbooks may also need to be provided.

An important design decision that has to be made at the start of a hypermedia project is whether the product is aimed at single or multiple types of user group (such as novices, experts, casual users and so on). This will influence whether or not a multi-level design strategy is needed and, if so, which 'user models' should be employed. At this stage some thought must also be given to access control with respect to who will be allowed to read information from the application and who will be allowed to write information to it.

In order that users can easily understand and use a hypermedia product they must be supplied with an appropriate 'model' of its structure and behaviour. This model will usually be provided by means of the various 'metaphors' that are embedded within the application. The role of metaphors in the design of hypermedia products is further discussed later in this section.

Information chunking
As we saw in the development model presented in Figure 2.6, an important aspect of design is the specification of the content and structure of the knowledge corpus that underlies the hypermedia application. Once the content has been decided upon, the basic material that is embedded within the knowledge corpus must be organized into appropriately sized units (or 'chunks') for presentation to users as and when they are needed. The process by which this is achieved is called 'chunking'. Usually, each chunk of

information will be represented by a node in the hypermedia knowledge corpus. The type, size and interrelationship of information chunks are important design considerations.

The chunks or nodes of information used in a hypermedia application can contain text, pictures or sound. They can also be of a multimedia nature, for example, text plus sound; text and pictures; sound and pictures, and so on. An example of a multimedia node is illustrated in Figure 1.4; an example of a pure text node is presented in Figure 1.5. Usually, chunking applies to text and sound but it can also be used with image-based material.

A given corpus of information can be divided into either a large number of small chunks or a small number of large chunks. The term used to identify this issue is called 'granularity'. Hypermedia structures with a large number of small chunks are called fine-grained; structures with very few large nodes are called coarse-grained.

A large number of small nodes can cause disorientation problems. On the other hand, a small number of large nodes can lead to specificity problems when indexing or retrieval tools are used. An optimum size for textual chunks would seem to be about two or three paragraphs (Begoray, 1990).

Linking
The linking strategy that is used within a given hypermedia product will depend upon the particular requirements of the application involved. A range of different link possibilities can exist depending upon:

● how many targets a button can link to;
● how many buttons are linked to a given target;
● whether a button can simultaneously invoke multiple targets; and
● the types of links involved (Begoray, 1990).

Again, careful decisions need to be made about how many links are made available from within a particular hypermedia node − too many can lead to complexity and disorientation while too few results in limited end-user control, a lack of flexibility and the creation of very simplistic hypermedia structures.

End-user service and tools

An important aspect of hypermedia design is the provision of toolsets and support services that can be used to facilitate the successful use of a product by its users. Certain 'standard services' (such as a bookmark facility, a notepad, a back-tracking tool, and so on) should always be provided. Wherever possible, generic tools such as these should be augmented by appropriate product-specific tools. Therefore, an important aspect of hypermedia application design is deciding what other types of tool/service should be provided with any given product. In this context the use of metaphors is very important. By embedding an appropriate metaphor (or a set of metaphors) within a particular product it is possible to use them to design appropriate support tools and services. The 'desktop' metaphor is one of the most commonly used within many computing applications. Similarly, we have found the 'book' metaphor to be extremely useful. However, many other possibilities exist, such as museum metaphors, travel metaphors and so on. The use of appropriate metaphors (and models based upon them) can prove to be a very successful design approach for the provision of toolsets and end-user services for hypermedia products.

End-user interface design

Because hypermedia systems are interactive and involve information display (on a CRT screen) and user control (through buttons and a pointing mechanism) considerable attention must be given to the design of the end-user interface to a hypermedia system. This section briefly reviews some of the important issues relating to end-user interface design. More detailed treatments of interface design are given in Barker (1989b) and Shneiderman (1992b).

Screen design

As has been described in Chapter 2, the use of a high-resolution screen is essential for the effective implementation of hypermedia. The screen is important because it must be used both for information display and for end-user control, through menus, buttons and icons.

Information will usually be displayed in both textual and

graphical forms, either individually or simultaneously, in appropriately designed 'windows'. A window is a section of the overall CRT screen area that has been allocated for the display of a particular piece of information. It is possible for many windows to exist simultaneously within the CRT screen area. Considerable thought must therefore be given to their size, shape, appearance and spatial properties (such as position, movability and re-sizability), Obviously, window design is a very important aspect of the end-user interface.

Menu bars and icons (for representing system tools and resources) are also an important design consideration. These will need to be designed and placed in an appropriate screen location that enables them to be easily accessed when they are needed. Generally, a wide range of menu techniques is available to choose from (such as horizontal and vertical menu bars, pull-down menus, pop-up menus, and so on), depending upon the type of authoring tool that is employed. Another useful method of allowing users to input information is through a 'dialogue box'; again, this needs to be designed with care so that its function is clear.

Other important design considerations that need to be taken into account include: the appropriate and consistent use of colour; an appropriate choice of text attributes (size, style, font and so on); provision of orientation information; and consistent screen layout within a given application.

Support for audio
In many hypermedia applications audio support will be needed. This can take a variety of different forms such as musical accompaniment, audio narrations, talking dictionaries and so on. The various types of sound effect that can be used will normally fall into two basic categories: mandatory and optional. Mandatory sound effects usually form an integral and necessary part of a particular presentation to which a user must listen. In contrast, the choice of listening to optional sound effects is usually left to the discretion of the user. The presence of optional sound resources within a hypermedia node will normally need to be indicated by the presence of on-screen icons (such as a 'loudspeaker', an 'ear' or a 'pair of headphones') that can also be used to access them. If a user elects to listen to an optional sound resource then additional icons

or buttons will also need to be provided to enable end-user control of the audio presentation. Possible control options include: repeating a segment, jumping ahead, exiting and changing the volume level. Controls of this sort will also be needed for the control of mandatory sound effects.

Button design

A button is essentially a reactive screen area that users can click on in order to cause some activity to take place, such as linking to another chunk of information, selecting a tool, exercising a control option or accessing information. Buttons for use in hypermedia systems can take a wide variety of forms (see Chapter 2) and the way in which an individual button is designed will depend upon the purpose it is to serve. The important design parameters that normally need to be considered when designing buttons are: visibility, shape, size, appearance and reactivity.

In Chapter 2 we identified three basic visibility states for a button – hidden, implicit and revealed. Essentially, the visibility attribute determines whether or not (and under what conditions) the presence of a button is made known to a user. The shape attribute is used to specify both the general shape class and more specific shape attributes. Most buttons will be of a rectangular shape (this is a general shape class) but some may be circular or polygonal. A rectangular button may have 'square' or 'rounded' corners and may (or may not) have a 'shadow' (these are specific shape parameters). The size of a button usually determines its reactive area and, thus, how easy it is to select it using a pointing operation – obviously, the larger the size of a button the fewer that can be fitted onto a screen. The appearance of a button depends upon its visual attributes such as its colour, transparency and label properties. Buttons may be labelled using text, picture segments, pictograms or audio messages. Buttons may also be multi-modal, multi-lingual and multi-cultural. The reactivity of a button will depend upon its function; usually, however, (at the very least) a button should give some 'feedback' to the user when it has been selected. Much of the documented knowledge relating to the design of menus and icons in human-computer interfaces will be very relevant and applicable to the design of buttons and hotspots for use in hypermedia applications (Barker, 1989b; Shneiderman, 1992b).

Using prototypes

Because hypermedia systems can be far more complex than conventional interactive systems, the 'linear' development model described earlier and shown in Figure 2.6 is frequently an inappropriate one to use. Instead, a cyclic, iterative development approach is often a more suitable one to adopt. Inherent in the use of this approach is the creation of a development 'prototype'. The role of such a prototype within the development cycle is illustrated schematically in Figure 3.1.

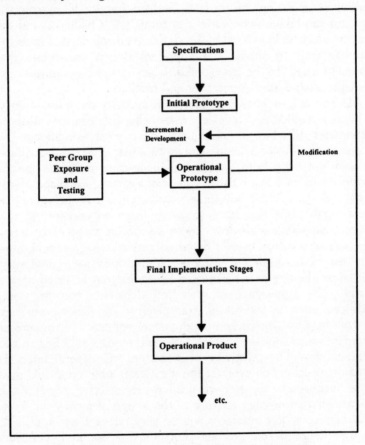

Figure 3.1 *Hypermedia development using a prototype*

Essentially, a prototype system is one which is constructed in order to explore and investigate the 'look and feel' of a product without having to undertake a complete system implementation. A prototype is therefore a partial implementation of a product which can be used to evaluate and test the basic system design and the appearance of a product before it is finally implemented. As can be seen from Figure 2.6, prototyping provides valuable feedback information about the underlying design of a system and, if necessary, this information can be used to modify the design prior to completing the final implementation.

Typically, a design team that is developing a hypermedia product would use a prototype system in order to test out their screen layouts, colour combinations, button designs, link strategies, interaction methodologies and various other design parameters on just a part of the system (using an appropriately chosen peer group). Then, if there are any obvious changes that need to be made these can be undertaken before the final stages of implementation get underway. The use of a prototype can therefore be used to circumvent mistakes that may otherwise be costly to correct.

When building a prototype it is important to use a suitable 'prototyping tool', that is, an authoring facility that enables a prototype to be created quickly and effectively. Software tools such as HyperCard and ToolBook are often used for the rapid construction of prototypes. Of course, the tool that is used to develop the prototype might also be used for the implementation of the final operational product. However, this need not necessarily be so; any of a wide spectrum of tools may be used for this purpose. Authoring tools are discussed in more detail later in this chapter.

Object orientation

The concept of object oriented design and fabrication was briefly mentioned earlier in the introduction to this chapter. Fundamental to this approach is the idea that we regard a hypermedia knowledge corpus as being composed of a collection of primitive reactive objects that constitute an 'object store'. This conceptualization is depicted graphically in the upper part of Figure 3.2 (Barker, 1992a). In this simple example the object store consists of just 20 basic objects each of which is labelled with a letter of the alphabet. These basic objects may be composed from text, sound or pictorial information, depending on how the corpus is defined and the purpose it is to serve. Each reactive object within an object store is able to participate in three basic types of activity: objects can receive messages from other objects; send messages to them; and perform various types of processing activity. As can be seen from Figure 3.2b, messages can come from different sources and can be sent to different destinations. The way in which an object reacts to any given input message (in terms of the processing activity that is initiated and the subsequent messages that it itself will send) will depend upon where the particular input message originates from.

Typically, within a hypermedia system, messages will be sent to and from a user via a mouse, keyboard and CRT screen. Essentially, each one of these entities is a system object that receives a message, transforms it in various ways and then passes it on to another system object. As an example of this, consider a situation in which a user is viewing a section of hypertext on a CRT screen and then decides to click on a particular hotspot within the display material. The material on the screen is essentially a message from an object (stored within the underlying object store) to the user – several messages (from other objects) may also be being displayed simultaneously, each within its own window area. When the user clicks the mouse button he or she is sending a message to the mouse which, in turn, sends a message to the object whose display has been selected. This object then sends a message to some other system object in order to satisfy the user's selection criteria.

Within the hypermedia systems that we design (some of these are discussed in more detail in Chapter 5) the basic objects that we create are composed from two basic parts: the display element and the interaction handler. The 'binary' structure of these objects is illustrated schematically in Figure 3.2C. The display material is essentially a message which, when the object is invoked, will be sent to a suitable display device such as a screen or an audio unit. The display message will normally embed buttons or hotspots to facilitate end-user control and interaction. These interactions (which are now essentially messages from a user) are handled by the interaction handler that is built into an object. The interaction handler is responsible for analysing messages coming from the user

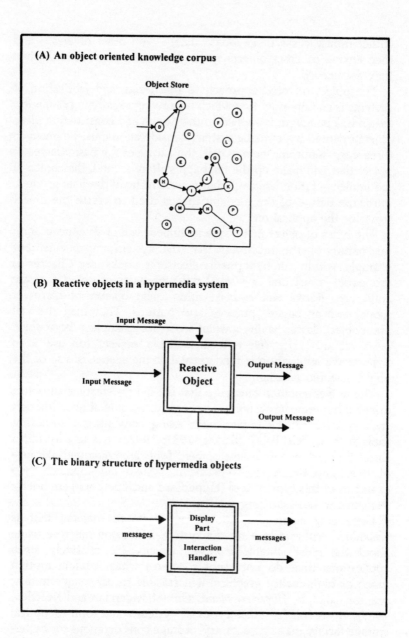

(A) An object oriented knowledge corpus

Object Store

(B) Reactive objects in a hypermedia system

Input Message

Input Message

Reactive Object

Output Message

Output Message

(C) The binary structure of hypermedia objects

messages

Display Part

Interaction Handler

messages

Figure 3.2 *Basic principle of the object oriented paradigm* (either mouse clicks or keyboard data) – and other objects – and then linking to other objects within the object store as and when they are needed.

The object oriented approach to the design and fabrication of systems is an important one which is growing rapidly in popularity. When this paradigm is applied to the design and construction of an object oriented hypermedia system, consideration must be given to three very important factors: first, the nature of the basic classes of object that will make up the final application; second, the choice of the implementation language that is used to build the final product; third, the nature of the medium that is used to create the object store for the application.

The types of object that a system embeds will often depend upon the nature of the metaphor that the system implements. For example, within our hypermedia electronic books (see Chapter 5) the 'book' is just one of several different types of object that are employed. Books will embed within them objects of narrower scope, such as 'pages', 'pictures' and 'buttons'. They may also call upon object classes having a wider scope, for example, a 'book shelf' or a 'library'. The selection of suitable objects for use in a hypermedia application is fundamental to the successful use of the object oriented paradigm.

The implementation language that is used for creating an object oriented hypermedia system is also a major consideration. Although such systems can be implemented using conventional authoring tools such as PC/PILOT (Barker, 1987; 1992a) it is usually much easier if object oriented development tools are employed. Because of their importance for hypermedia system development, two examples of this type of tool (HyperCard and ToolBook) are briefly described in the following section.

Depending upon the amount and type of material that is embedded within a hypermedia system, a decision must be made about the most suitable storage medium. For relatively small applications (that do not involve objects which contain motion video or high-quality graphics) it is feasible to use magnetic disc; see, for example, *Hypertext Hands On!* (Shneiderman and Kearsley, 1989). However, for other types of system some form of optical storage facility may be necessary. Storage considerations for hypermedia systems are discussed in more detail later in this chapter.

Authoring environments

A wide range of authoring environments currently exist for the creation of hypermedia resources. The origin of these tools is quite varied. Some of them have their roots in computer-assisted learning (Barker, 1987) or computer-based training (Dean and Whitlock, 1992) while others have originated from research and development into tools to support interactive documentation (Brown, 1986a) and non-linear information storage. Examples of some of the more well-known hypermedia authoring tools are listed in Table 3.1.

Undoubtedly, one of the most well-known, low-cost hypermedia development and delivery environments is the HyperCard system that runs on Apple Macintosh computers. As was suggested in Chapter 1, in many ways the relatively widespread availability of this system has done much to promote the popularity of hypertext

Table 3.1 *Some popular hypermedia authoring tools*

Tool	Platform
KnowledgePro	IBM PC
IconAuthor	IBM PC
PC/PILOT	IBM PC
PROPI	IBM PC
GUIDE	IBM PC and Macintosh
HYPERTIES	IBM PC
HyperCard	Macintosh
SuperCard	Macintosh
ToolBook	IBM PC
LinkWay	IBM PC
Authorware Professional	IBM PC and Macintosh
Lotus SmarText	IBM PC
HyperPAD	IBM PC
Hyperdoc	IBM PC
HyperNotes	IBM PC
HyperSprint	IBM PC
StackMaker	Macintosh

and hypermedia. SuperCard is similar to HyperCard but provides many extra facilities and also enhances some of the features that are only poorly catered for in HyperCard itself. The GUIDE system was probably one of the first commercially available hypertext packages for the IBM PC platform. HYPERTIES and KnowledgePro are two other early systems that became available for workstations based on IBM PC compatibles. KnowledgePro is useful since it also embeds an expert system facility and may therefore be used to develop 'intelligent' hypermedia systems. LinkWay is another, more recently available, authoring environment for IBM PCs.

As well as using special purpose tools for developing hypermedia it is also possible to use conventional programming languages (such as Pascal and C) and CBT authoring tools such as PC/PILOT and PROPI. Although languages like C can lead to very efficient implementations of hypermedia, development is often slow due to the time it takes to gain experience with them. Naturally, the ease of use of an authoring system and the repertoire of support tools that it provides will significantly influence the productivity of hypermedia authors. In this context, Barker (1992a) has illustrated how PC/PILOT can be used in a simple and effective way for the development of both hypertext and hypermedia systems.

The particular tool used to develop hypermedia resources for any given project will depend very much upon the nature of the project itself. In choosing a hypermedia development environment it is important to establish appropriate criteria by which candidate systems may be evaluated. An evaluation of some of the different tools for creating hypertext (on IBM PCs) has been conducted by Morrall (1991). She found that the HYPERTIES system came out best for the types of application in which she was interested (public browsing software for use in a museum). As mentioned earlier the object oriented approach to design and development is growing substantially in popularity. For this reason, many hypermedia authors now choose an authoring tool that embeds this paradigm, such as HyperCard or ToolBook. Because of their importance for developing hypermedia materials each of these systems is briefly described below.

HyperCard

A brief introduction to HyperCard has already been presented in Chapter 1. It was stated there that HyperCard screens could be used to model reactive notecards that could contain various types of multimedia information. A typical example of a multimedia card was presented in Figure 1.4. Collections of cards on a common theme are organized together into an organizational unit called a 'stack'. Stacks are usually represented by multimodal icons similar to those shown in the 'screen dump' presented in the upper part of Figure 3.3.

Each of the icons in this diagram is reactive in that any one of them can be selected and opened (by pointing to the one of interest

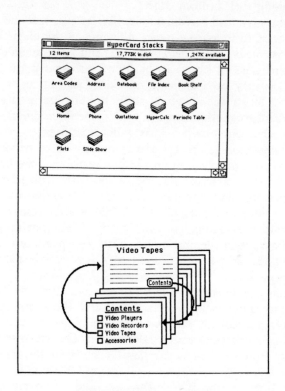

Figure 3.3 *HyperCard stacks*

and double clicking on it). When a stack is opened it becomes operational, that is, users can navigate through it and access the information held on its member cards. An example of a simple stack containing two basic types of card is illustrated schematically in the lower part of Figure 3.3 (Goodman, 1987).

Obviously, both cards and stacks are examples of HyperCard objects. Individual cards are themselves built up from three more fundamental types of object. Each card in a stack usually contains a background, one or more fields, and a set of buttons.

A background serves to contain decorative material (and other objects) that are common to a group of cards; Figure 2.9 shows the appearance of two cards having the same common background: a spiral running across the top of the cards and a set of filing tabs running along their bottom edge.

The fields on a card contain information (such as text and images) that is specific to individual cards. In Figure 1.4, for example, there are two basic fields: a text field on the left and a picture on the right.

The third class of object to be found on cards is the reactive button. This may be specific to an individual card or it may be common to all cards in a given stack. Buttons are used to move from one card to another within a stack or between different stacks – they are thus often used for navigation purposes.

Both the authoring process and some aspects of navigation in HyperCard are controlled by the options available in the horizontal menu bar that runs across the top of the Macintosh screen. This menu bar, along with the pull-down option lists that each makes available, is illustrated in Figure 3.4. As can be seen from this figure, facilities exist for creating, copying, saving, deleting and protecting stacks. Stacks can be protected both by password and by controlling the access rights given to a user. Cards can also be created, copied and deleted.

The tools palette embeds a range of different functions. There are tools for creating fields and buttons and there are tools for generating graphics on cards and for entering text into textual fields. Whenever a paint tool is selected, the 'Objects' menu option disappears from the menu bar and is replaced by three extra painting menu options ('Paint', 'Options' and 'Patterns').

The options in the 'Go' menu are used for navigation; for example, the options 'First', 'Prev', 'Next' and 'Last' cause jumps to

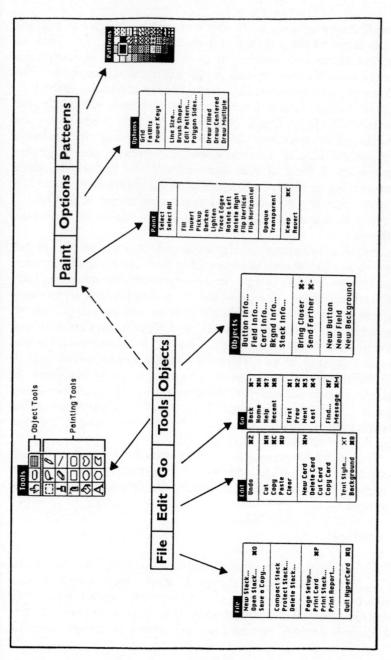

Figure 3.4 *HyperCard menu options*

the first card in a stack, the previous card to the current one, the next card and the last card in a stack, respectively. The 'Find ...' option allows text searches to be performed, such as finding the next card in the current stack containing the word 'hypertext'. The 'Message' option allows the user to type in commands directly to the HyperCard system; a typical interactive command might be: Go to card ID 5127 of stack 'Helper'. The 'Objects' menu allows the author of a stack to obtain information about the different HyperCard objects it contains and, if necessary, to change the properties of these objects. Some examples of the way in which information on HyperCard objects is held is illustrated in Figure 3.5. Notice that the button objects themselves embed a 'LinkTo ...' button that enables them to be linked to other card and stack objects.

Another important button contained in each of the object representations shown in Figure 3.5 is the 'Script ...' button which enables an object's 'script' to be examined and modified. Each HyperCard object is represented by a script which is executed whenever the object is invoked. Scripts are written using an object oriented programming language called HyperTalk (Coulouris and Thimbleby, 1992; Shafer, 1988). HyperTalk is used to define the basic properties of each HyperCard object and to specify how it should behave when it receives a message from another object. A simple example of a HyperTalk script for a button is illustrated in Table 3.2. This script embeds three event handlers which define how a particular button should react to different messages sent to it by the system's mouse.

HyperCard stacks can be used to implement a wide range of interactive applications. As we shall discuss in the following chapter, their use as educational and training resources is particularly important.

ToolBook

The ToolBook system has been developed by the Asymetrix Corporation (Asymetrix, 1989a). In many ways this authoring environment is very similar to the HyperCard system which was described in the previous section. Indeed, like HyperCard, the ToolBook system provides a very powerful object oriented

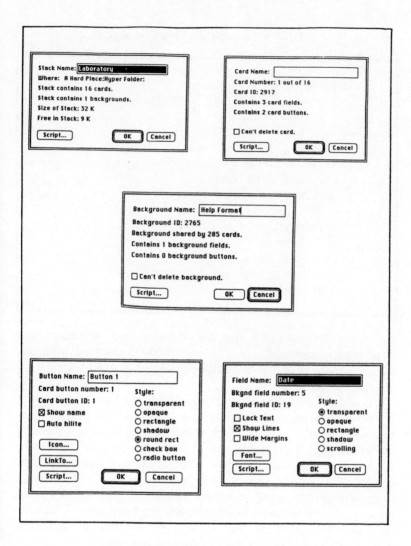

Figure 3.5 *Information on HyperCard objects*

Table 3.2 *Example of a HyperCard script*

```
on mouseDown
     put "Down" into Message
     wait 40
     put 0 into Message
end mouseDown
on mouseStillDown
     add 10 to Message
end mouseStillDown

on mouseUp
     beep 3
     wait 20
     put "Done" into Message
end mouseUp
```

authoring environment for the development of interactive hypermedia resources. The underlying object oriented programming language upon which ToolBook is based is called 'OpenScript' (Asymetrix, 1989b).

ToolBook runs on IBM PC platforms within a Microsoft Windows environment. As its name suggests, ToolBook implements a 'book' metaphor. Each screen of information generated using ToolBook is called a page and a collection of pages then make up a book. Individual pages of a book can embed various combinations of text, graphics, control facilities and collections of reactive buttons. Some examples of typical pages taken from various interactive books that have been produced using ToolBook are illustrated in Figure 3.6. These serve to illustrate both the general structure and layout of pages and the nature of the graphical user interface within which they are displayed and used.

The ToolBook environment provides two basic levels of access for users: reader level and author level. At reader level it is possible to flip through and add pages to a book; to type, edit and format text in fields; and to print out sections of a book. The menu bar options available at reader level are illustrated in Figure 3.6A; they

A: ToolBook at Reader Level

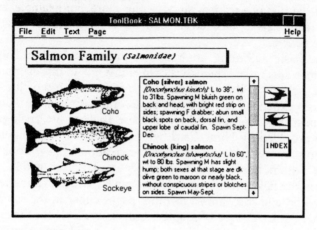

B: ToolBook at Author Level

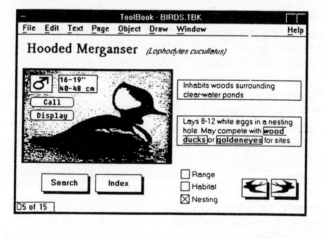

Figure 3.6 *Examples of ToolBook pages*

are: File, Edit, Text, Page and Help. At author level more menu options are available (see Figure 3.6B). At this level it is possible to do all the things a reader can do – plus more. For example, authors can create new books, create and modify objects on pages and create scripts.

The basic authoring environment presented by the ToolBook system is illustrated schematically in Figure 3.7. In this diagram each of the options in the horizontal menu bar at the top of the screen has been expanded to reflect the types of facility that the ToolBook system makes available. Many of these facilities are analogous to those provided by HyperCard (which are illustrated in Figure 3.4).

Tools are available to facilitate the creation of new books, new pages within books and various types of object within pages. Within text fields, words and phrases can be marked, converted into 'hotwords' and then linked to other pages either in the same or in another book. A range of graphics tools is available for the creation of graphic objects. These may be of two different types: draw objects and paint objects. A draw object is a graphics shape created with one of the drawing tools and stored as mathematical data describing its position and appearance. A paint object is an object created by pasting a bitmap onto a page; the bitmap is usually obtained using a scanner or an external paint program.

One very useful ToolBook application that can be loaded into ToolBook is the 'Bookshelf' facility – in some ways this is similar to the 'home card' in HyperCard. A screen dump of a typical Bookshelf is illustrated schematically in Figure 3.8. Each book within the Bookshelf is represented by a multimodal icon; when a particular icon is selected and invoked (using a mouse) its corresponding book is opened – notice the similarity between ToolBook's books and HyperCard's stacks.

As was the case in HyperCard, each object in ToolBook is represented by a script. A script is a series of OpenScript statements, or instructions, that tell an object what to do. Some examples of typical ToolBook scripts are listed in Table 3.3. Every object in ToolBook can have a script, including hotwords, groups (a group is a collection of other objects), graphics, fields, pages, backgrounds and books themselves. The script for an object is divided into logical parts called 'handlers' which describe what should happen when a specific event occurs, such as a reader

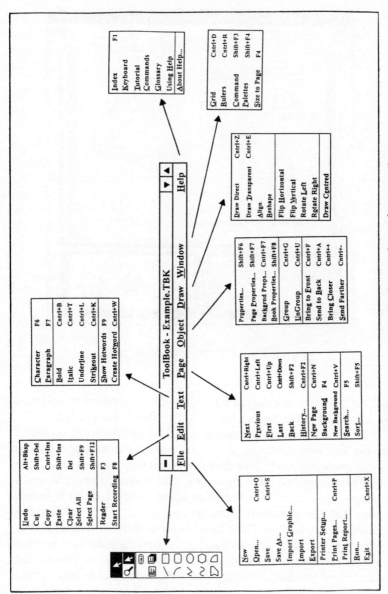

Figure 3.7 *Format of the ToolBook menu bar and menu options*

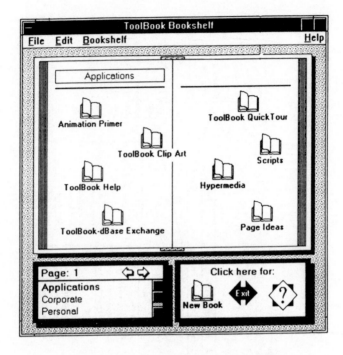

Figure 3.8 *The ToolBook 'Bookshelf' facility*

clicking a button or pressing a key. ToolBook responds to an event by running the handler for that event in the object's script.

If an object receives a message and its script does not contain a handler for that message, ToolBook passes the message up the 'object hierarchy' until it finds a corresponding handler for it. The object hierarchy, shown in Figure 3.9, determines the order in which messages are passed from object to object until a handler is found. Notice that the Windows Dynamic Link Library (DLL) facility can be used to extend ToolBook in all sorts of different ways. This is achieved by writing DLL entries for controlling software modules that can run and control various add-on facilities such as digital video, sound production equipment, other applications and so on.

Like HyperCard, the ToolBook system is growing rapidly in popularity for implementing educational applications of hypermedia. Some interesting applications of ToolBook for instructional

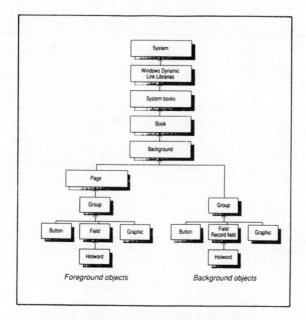

Figure 3.9 *Object hierarchy in ToolBook*

purposes have been described by Ingraham and Emery (1991) and by Beilby (1992). The first of these discusses the use of ToolBook for developing hypermedia courseware to support interactive foreign language teaching (French) while the second explores its potential as a general authoring environment for academic material. We have been using ToolBook for the implementation of various sorts of electronic book. Some of our work in this area is described later in Chapter 5.

Storage and delivery technologies

When the basic design and development of a hypermedia product is complete, some thought must be given to how it will be made available to users. A range of possibilities exist, depending on the actual size of the product, the storage medium that is employed for its underlying knowledge corpus and the delivery platform that is to be used in order to access it. Three of the most commonly used

Table 3.3 *Examples of ToolBook scripts*

```
to handle buttonUp
      step i from 4660 to 3260 by -100
      set bounds of rectangle "rect1" to 1185,i,1599,5080
end step

      step i from 4660 to 2460 by -100
      et bounds of rectangle "rect2" to 1672,i,2086,5080
end step

      step i from 4660 to 2960 by -100
      set bounds of rectangle "rect3" to 2144,i,2558,5080
end step
      . .
      . .
      . .
end buttonUp
```

```
to handle enterBook
      put sysTime into text of field "time"
      if "am" is in sysTime
            set visible of group "GoodMorning" to true
            pause 3 seconds
            set visible of group "goodMorning" to false
      else
            set visible of group "greetings" to true
            pause 3 seconds
            set visible of group "greetings" to false
      end if
end enterBook
```

```
to handle buttonUp
      set SysDateFormat to "m/d/y"
      get sysDate
      put sysDate into text of field "currDate"
end buttonUp

to handle buttonDown
      show field "popup1"
end buttonDown

to handle buttonDoubleClick
      local x,y
      step x from 1000 to 5000 by 500
            step y from 2000 to 5000 by 500
                  move group "frame" to x,y
            end step
      end step
end buttonDoubleClick
```

access strategies are: distribute, install and deliver; distribute and deliver directly; and remote access. Each of these is briefly discussed below.

The distribution process involves the physical movement of a product from the development environment across to the host environment that is provided by a user's workstation. In order to achieve this, some form of 'transfer' mechanism is needed. The usual way of transferring material is by means of a suitable storage medium such as magnetic or optical disc. Alternatively, if a communication network is available (and the delivery station can be attached to it) then direct transfer from the development environment to the delivery environment may be possible. When hypermedia material arrives at the host delivery station it may need to be installed before it can be used. Installation, if this is necessary, involves transferring the product from the distribution medium into the user's workstation ready for use. Depending upon what is involved, installation can be quite a complex and time-consuming process. Once a product has been installed it can be delivered. The delivery process actually involves users directly interacting with the product in order to obtain information of interest.

Sometimes, hypermedia products can be distributed in a form that enables them to be delivered directly without the need for any installation procedures. The success of this 'distribute and deliver' approach depends very much upon the size of the knowledge corpus involved, the type of material that it embeds and the nature of the distribution medium that is used.

Another useful way of accessing a hypermedia product is by means of remote access. This involves making a product available on a suitable host computer system that can be accessed by users through the use of a telecommunications network. Usually, the host computer will be a large time-sharing mainframe computer or minicomputer system that is capable of supporting many simultaneous users. The advantage of this approach is that there is neither a distribution phase nor any form of installation necessary.

In order to realize the hypermedia access methods described above, three basic storage and delivery technologies are normally employed: computer-based communications networks; magnetic media; and optical storage media. The potential of each of these is briefly discussed in the remainder of this section.

Using communications networks

As was suggested above, computer-based communications networks provide two extremely useful methods of making hypermedia material available: remote access and distribution (or 'downloading') in electronic form. In order to use either (or both) of these approaches, appropriate communications resources must be made available to and within the delivery station. One of the most common ways of connecting a delivery station to a remote computer is by means of a 'modem'. This is a device that converts computer-based information into a form that can be transmitted over a conventional telephone line. Establishing a connection between a delivery station and a remote host (the source of hypermedia material) is then simply a matter of 'dialling' the remote host's telephone number, logging on to the host and then either accessing or downloading the relevant hypermedia resources.

Using magnetic media

The most common form of magnetic medium for distributing hypermedia resources is the 'floppy disc'. Discs come in a variety of different sizes and storage capacities. The major limitation of such discs is the relatively small amount of storage that they make available (about two megabytes). Transfer speed (from the disc into the delivery station) may also be a problem in some cases. In order to overcome the storage capacity problem, large amounts of material are usually distributed in compressed form. Material in this format is normally decompressed and installed on a hard disc within the delivery station. The hypermedia material is then delivered from the hard disc upon which it has been installed. The hypermedia material that accompanies the book *Hypertext Hands-On!*, for example, is distributed on floppy discs for installation on, and delivery from, a hard disc (Shneiderman and Kearsley, 1989).

Another useful magnetic medium for distributing hypermedia material is the 'tape streamer'. This is a high capacity magnetic tape facility that can be used to transfer very large volumes of material from one location to another. The disadvantage of this approach is that it requires a special hardware unit in order to transfer material to the tape and, subsequently, install it within the delivery station.

Using optical storage

Four basic types of optical storage media are commonly used for storing hypermedia materials during the development and/or distribution phases of a project: analogue video disc; rewritable (magneto-optical) optical disc; write-once read-many (WORM) discs; and compact disc read-only memory (CD-ROM).

Video disc is a popular way of storing static pictures and motion video segments for use in a hypermedia production. Substantial volumes of high-quality pictorial material can be stored on this medium. Usually, when used in a hypermedia system the images (or video segments) that are retrieved from a video disc are converted into digital form. They can then be manipulated in various ways and subsequently displayed within a suitably sized window on the CRT screen of the delivery station (alongside other material).

Video discs are a 'read only' medium. That is, once information has been placed on a disc it cannot be changed. Unlike video discs, magneto-optical discs store information in a digital fashion and they can be updated (that is, stored information can be changed). Unfortunately, because of their expense, discs of this sort are not normally employed for distributing hypermedia resources. Such discs are usually only used for 'back-up' purposes and for product testing during the prototyping phase of a hypermedia project.

WORM discs are another popular way of distributing digital information. Although existing information on discs of this type cannot be altered, they can be updated by using any unused space that they contain. WORM discs form the basis of 'Photo CD' – a new process that enables photographs and slides to be stored on compact disc (CD) and subsequently viewed on a TV screen.

CD-ROM is undoubtedly one of the most popular storage media for hypermedia resources. Examples of the ways in which this medium can be used have been given by a number of authors; see, for example, Barker and Giller (1991); Bogaerts and Agema (1992); Britannica Software (1990; 1991); and Megarry (1988; 1991). The attractive feature of CD-ROM is its substantial storage capacity (typically 650 megabytes) enabling large amounts of textual, pictorial and audio material to be stored. Provided that suitable compression and decompression techniques are used, CD-ROM can also be used to store motion video segments. A variety of different types of delivery platform based upon CD-ROM are now emerging. Some of the most well-known are CD-I (compact disc-interactive), CD-ROM XA (compact disc-extended architecture) and CDTV (Commodore's Dynamic Total Vision). CD-ROM can also be used with DVI (digital video interactive) for the provision of motion video using compression and decompression techniques based upon special 'boards' that can be inserted within a PC-based delivery station. Some of these delivery platforms (and products based on them) will be discussed later.

Conclusion

A variety of different tools and techniques are needed in order to produce effective hypermedia materials. This chapter has attempted to outline some of the basic requirements needed in order to undertake a successful hypermedia project. Undoubtedly, five of the most important 'stepping stones' to success in this area are:

- selecting an appropriate design paradigm;
- adopting a suitable development methodology;
- adhering to relevant design guidelines (where these are available);
- using appropriate development tools; and
- selecting the most effective and efficient mechanism for enabling users to access the final product.

Bearing in mind these five points, in much of our work we have found the use of an object oriented approach to be highly beneficial, especially when it is used in conjunction with authoring tools such as HyperCard and ToolBook that support this method of working. In the context of development methodology, we strongly recommend the use of an iterative approach based upon the use of a prototype. Much of our experience suggests that this is a very useful way of proceeding, especially when there are few guidelines available to help steer the direction of development.

Finally, with respect to giving users access to hypermedia products, we have found two approaches useful: first, the use of a local area network to which are attached a large number of interactive delivery stations (such an arrangement enables hypermedia resources to be downloaded to individual workstations in a classroom situation); second, the use of CD-ROM discs. The use of CD-ROM is likely to grow substantially in the future in order to meet increased demand for portability of resources.

The first three chapters of this book have attempted to explain the meaning of hypermedia, its background and how it can be developed. In the remaining three chapters we shall proceed to explore ways in which this important technology can be used to support education and training in both formal and informal situations.

4 Educational Perspective

Introduction

As we have established in previous chapters, hypertext and hypermedia are made possible by the facilities provided by modern interactive computer systems, particularly the high-resolution display screens and the various types of pointing device that they employ. The use of such computer systems as an instructional resource has grown substantially over the last decade. There are two main reasons for this: first, the fact that computing has become a major part of the taught curriculum within schools, colleges and universities; second, the realization that computers can be used (with considerable success) to augment and improve conventional teaching and learning processes (Barker, 1989c; Kibby and Hartley, 1992).

To date, there has been little well-documented evidence to suggest that hypertext and hypermedia can be used to improve teaching and learning processes in a very substantial way at all levels of the curriculum. Despite this, and for a variety of reasons, there is a growing number of educational applications that now use the non-linear information delivery mechanisms that this approach embeds. Undoubtedly, within most educational organizations the popularity of hypermedia was originally sparked off by the availability of (relatively) low-cost personal computer systems (such as the Apple Macintosh) which came 'bundled' with software packages (such as HyperCard) that could enable non-technical users to prepare interactive courseware with minimal effort. Nowadays, virtually all interactive computing platforms provide 'easy to use' tools to facilitate the development of instructional software to support teaching and learning applications of computers.

Unfortunately, conventional courseware often suffers from many serious limitations. One of its chief drawbacks is its lack of flexibility and its inability to adapt to the particular needs of individual users. In principle, one of the major advantages of 'hyper-courseware' is that it can be designed in such a way that many of the limitations of conventional courseware can be overcome (Siviter and Brown, 1992). Other advantages that are claimed for hypermedia courseware include greater learner control; improved access to multimedia learning materials; and a variety of new modalities of interaction for use with learning material (Hutchings *et al.*, 1992).

Obviously, if hypermedia material is to be educationally effective considerable thought must be given to:

- the learning goals and activities that it must support;
- how the nature of the underlying knowledge corpus relates to these requirements; and
- how learners will differ from each other.

Bearing these factors in mind, a major task must then be the design of appropriate support tools to facilitate the creation of and access to hypermedia knowledge corpora.

In this chapter we shall explore some of the educational possibilities of hypertext and hypermedia materials. We commence by examining more closely some of the issues mentioned above. Then, we consider some different kinds of application areas for educational hypermedia – in the classroom, in the workplace and in the home. The chapter concludes with a selection of short descriptive case studies that illustrate some of the interesting ways in which instructional hypermedia techniques are being applied in a variety of different situations and contexts.

Fundamental issues

As we suggested above, a range of different issues have to be considered when designing hypermedia material for educational applications. One of the most important factors to consider (and understand) is the type of educational application for which the resources are intended. Because of its importance this issue is discussed in considerable detail later in the chapter. However, before undertaking this discussion, it is necessary to 'set the scene' by presenting some of the important background issues that need to be understood in order to design and use hypermedia resources for instructional purposes.

Basic background considerations

When attempting to answer the question 'What makes educationally effective hypermedia material?', Hutchings *et al.* (1992) identified three factors which they thought had a major influence on the quality of an educational hypermedia product. They used the terms 'control', 'engagement' and 'synthesis' to refer to these factors.

Control refers to the degree to which the learner rather than the system controls exposure to the learning materials, the particular learning activity and the delivery strategy that is employed. Engagement refers to the extent to which learners can process the hypermedia materials actively rather than passively. Synthesis refers to the nature of the learning activity: does it require the learner to create materials or relationships rather than merely observe them? Hutchings *et al.* suggested that these three factors (control, engagement and synthesis) can be used to define a cube similar to that shown in Figure 4.1.

By dividing each axis of this cube into two, a simple eight-region taxonomy of hypermedia systems can be defined. Within this taxonomy the region at the left, lower back represents basic hypertext systems (since they typically allow learner control, passive engagement and simple presentation of materials). Progressing along the dimensions, at the opposite side of the cube are hypermedia materials that involve active engagement and creativity by the learner. Typical examples of active and creative tasks in which learners might become involved include self-generated tours; the use of annotation facilities; the creation of concept maps; preparing multimedia essays and reports; doing 'knowledge jigsaws'; browsing; retrieving; editing; updating; reporting; problem-solving; and co-working with other students (either locally or remotely).

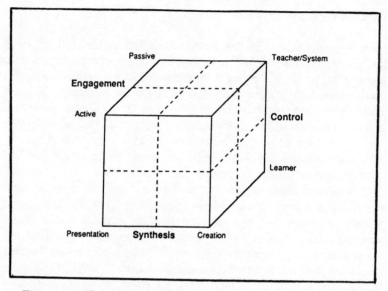

Figure 4.1 *Three important design dimensions for educational hypermedia*

Based upon the cube shown in Figure 4.1, Hutchings *et al.* (1992) have suggested that the construction of hypermedia systems should move as quickly as possible from the passive, browse-only mode which most systems incorporate. They suggest that authors should think in terms of a network of different kinds of activity involving, for example, simulation, modelling and problem-solving tasks.

Another important point to remember when designing learning strategies for using computers in teaching is that 'deep learning' will usually take place away from the machine, during periods of reflection, discussion with colleagues, writing and active attempts at explanation. Obviously, this observation provides another reason for making computer-based activities involving hypermedia as interesting, exciting and attractive as possible, so that, hopefully, students will take away with them useful memories of their encounters with the system.

Use of metaphors

The use of metaphors has been mentioned on several previous occasions in this book. Their use in human–computer interface design and in various types of learning product is well-documented in the literature (Carroll *et al.*, 1988). The main advantage of using metaphors (both in the design of a product and in subsequent interaction with it) lies in the 'cognitive transfer' that is associated with their use. That is, in a learning situation, students can carry across knowledge and skills relevant to one (well-known or familiar) domain and use them in another less familiar area.

A range of different types of metaphor has been proposed and used in the development of hypermedia resources for educational purposes. Sometimes, the learning product embeds just a single metaphor, but often, several metaphors are 'mixed' within the same application. Four interesting types of metaphor that are finding increasing utility in hypermedia design are the 'story', the 'guide', the 'museum' and the 'book'. Each of these is briefly described below.

The use of stories as a design metaphor for hypertext (and hypermedia) has been advocated quite strongly by McLellan (1992; 1993). She suggests that 'stories represent an enduring and appealing mechanism for communicating information especially in an instructional context.' McLellan argues that there are three important reasons for using stories as a basis for instructional design in hypertext: first, they provide a familiar and well-known information structure; second, they can reduce the cognitive load imposed by navigating through a wealth of information; third, they offer covert interactivity through cognitive and imaginative engagement. Laurel (1991) also suggests that a 'dramatic model' for story-telling in a computer environment offers many benefits in terms of engagement and emotion that enhance the experience of the human participant.

The use of travel metaphors or guides applied to a learning domain is another important way of organizing and structuring information within a hypermedia system. This approach has been described in detail by a number of developers such as Hammond and Allinson (1987) and Oren *et al.* (1990). The success of this approach depends upon the designer's ability to create a number of guided tours or pathways through the learning material that the user can choose from.

The museum metaphor likens a hypermedia knowledge corpus to a collection of 'exhibits' which one might expect to find in a real museum. Users are free to browse through the museum in an ad hoc fashion; they can also investigate particular themes of interest or participate in any of a number of guided tours similar to those described above. One practical implementation of the museum metaphor can be found in the hypermedia compact disc publication entitled 'Treasures of the Smithsonian', a description of which is presented later in this chapter.

The book metaphor is another that is quite extensively used. Here, the hypermedia knowledge corpus is regarded as a collection of reactive pages of electronic information that is displayed upon the screen of a TV or a CRT display device. Reactive objects in any given page are linked to one or more other objects which can be activated whenever the need arises. Examples of the use of this metaphor are well-documented in the literature (Asymetrix, 1989a; 1989b; Barker, 1992b; 1992c) – some of these are described later in this chapter. We shall return to a more detailed discussion of the book metaphor in the following chapter which deals with hypermedia electronic books.

Styles of learning

One very important consideration that needs to be taken into account when designing educational materials is the style of learning that any given student is likely to adopt during a particular learning transaction. The preferred ways in which students choose to learn are often referred to by the term 'learning style' (Entwistle, 1981; Ford, 1985; Pask, 1976). Learning styles can vary quite considerably. For example, in a conventional group learning situation, some students will prefer to attend lecture presentations while others will show a preference for small-group interactive teaching/learning. Similarly, in an individualized learning situation some students will opt for learning from books or computers while many others will prefer to acquire their knowledge as a result of practical experience.

Of course, the learning styles that people use are by no means rigid or fixed: it is possible for individuals to change their learning style depending upon their mood, the type of material that is to be assimilated and the particular situation that they happen to be in. For example, in some situations a particular individual might prefer to listen to a spoken exposition on a topic, while on another occasion (in a different situation) that same person might prefer to read about the topic or watch a TV programme about it. Obviously, situations of this type can create difficult design problems for hypermedia designers if total system flexibility is desired.

Ideally, a truly flexible and adaptive hypermedia system should be capable of performing very detailed monitoring of its individual users. The system should be able to record, in different situations, its users' misconceptions and preferred modes of system access, information presentation and learning styles. Subsequently, such a system should be able to adapt (dynamically and automatically) to a particular user's needs at any given instant. Unfortunately, few if any systems are currently able to do this successfully because of the very complex nature of the computer software that is needed and a less than good understanding of the psychology of learning. However, despite this, it is certainly feasible for designers to be aware of the different 'learning styles' possibilities that exist and then to build hypermedia systems that are able to accommodate these. Users of such systems would then be able to choose for themselves which particular style they prefer at any given time.

From what has been said above, it should be apparent that the creation of hypermedia products for instructional purposes requires that consideration should be given to a range of complex 'learning styles' decisions. For example, a designer will need to select the level(s) at which a given topic will be treated; this may range from extremely shallow to very deep. Considerable thought must also be given to the types of presentation strategy that will be used, ranging from linear through pseudo-linear to highly non-linear. The basic learning approaches that are used must also be decided upon; these might be prescriptive, exploratory or based upon guided discovery learning and/or assessment. Decisions will also need to be made on whether or not any form of assessment is used and, if so, what form this should take. Related to this last decision is the choice of level(s) and type(s) of feedback that will be provided by the system. Another very important decision that will need to be taken early on in a project will concern the nature of the 'primary' and 'secondary' communication channels that will be used (the modes of these might be textual, audio or graphical).

Obviously, when designing educational hypermedia a complex set of design decisions have to be made. It is therefore important that appropriate models and guidelines are made available to system designers in order to help them make the right decisions. There are many useful sources of information now available to enable designers to make informed decisions about hypermedia in a learning context; some examples include: Horn (1989); Jonassen and Mandl (1990); Landow (1989b) and Shneiderman (1989).

Another important consideration that must be taken into account when designing hypermedia systems for educational use is the type(s) of user who will ultimately use the system. Because of its importance this issue is briefly discussed in the following section.

Types of learner

A consideration of the 'types of learner' that will use an educational hypermedia environment is important because this factor will often strongly influence the learning styles that it should support. A number of different ways of classifying 'hypermedia learners' currently exist. The simplest taxonomy is one which contains just two basic classes of learner: non-discretionary and discretionary.

Non-discretionary learners have no choice about whether or not they will use a hypermedia package – they have to, since there will usually be no other way of acquiring the knowledge or skills that are embedded within it. An example of such non-discretionary use is a situation in which an employee has to learn about a new piece of equipment and the associated instructional material is provided in the form of a hypermedia training package; no other training material is provided. In contrast, discretionary users will be able to exercise a choice between using such a package and not using it; usually, alternative forms of training will be available. Obviously, for this latter type of learner, if a hypermedia package is not well-designed and produced at a level appropriate for the people who are intended to use it, then it will simply not get used; people will acquire the skills they need in other ways.

Another important way of classifying learners relates to the level of experience they have with respect to the subject domain being presented. In this taxonomy the two extreme cases are 'novices' and 'experts'. Each of these types of learner will have different requirements and expectations and so the hypermedia system must be designed accordingly. Usually, if both types of learner are to be accommodated within a single product then different 'trails' through the knowledge corpus must be planned. This will therefore necessitate the creation of a 'multi-level' hypermedia system. This possibility is discussed in more detail later.

Other important learner dimensions that should be taken into account when designing a hypermedia product include: age, sex, educational level, prior training, ethnic background, cultural heritage, level of motivation, personality and physical abilities. Each one of these factors can significantly influence the success of a hypermedia system and its acceptability in the eyes of its user population. A knowledge and understanding of the types of learner that will use an educational hypermedia product is even more important when it is aimed at an international audience. For example, one large European hypermedia development project called 'Hypermedia for Teaching' (Barker, 1993a) involves producing a teaching package for distribution throughout the member states of the European Community; the material is required to be available in six different languages and must cater for many different types of learner. Obviously, the design problems involved in catering for such a large disparate group of users are immense. The way in which these problems are overcome and further details of this project are presented later in this chapter.

Educational applications of hypermedia

As we suggested at the beginning of this chapter, the use of hypermedia techniques is starting to appear in educational materials in a variety of different ways, some more obvious than others. Typical examples include HyperCard stacks for use in schools and colleges, shared hypermedia knowledge corpora that can be accessed by various educational and training organizations; specific products aimed at the consumer market; and software products aimed specifically at computer users. Obviously, in most situations the way in which the hypermedia technique is used will depend very much on the characteristics of the 'learner population' for which the product is intended. In the following three sections of this chapter three different types of learning situation are considered: learners who are situated in some form of 'classroom' environment; those who may be in a workplace situation; and those in a home environment.

Hypermedia in the classroom

The potential of hypermedia in a classroom environment has been discussed by a number of different authors who between them consider each level of the curriculum. Barker and Giller (1991) for example, describe the use of a hypermedia package (distributed on compact disc) for use by early learners. This package embeds an electronic book metaphor and is based upon the letters of the alphabet. Young learners can select any particular letter by touching a reactive CRT screen. They can then look at pictures of objects whose names begin with the selected letter; they can also listen to the names of the objects, which can be spoken in any of several European languages. For children who can read, hypertext stories are available – as well as interactive games! Although some evaluation of the educational impact of this system was undertaken, this was not a major concern in this project; the main issue was to explore how hypermedia materials might be used in a classroom environment.

Evaluation of educational impact was of more concern in the middle school hypertext reading study conducted by Horney in his 'ElectroText Project' (Horney and Anderson-Inman, 1993). He studied the hypertext reading strategies employed by middle school children in different task orientated situations. He observed that children employed any of six different reading patterns – skimming, checking, reading, responding, studying and reviewing – depending upon the situation in which they were placed. Unfortunately, no clear cut support for the positive effects of hypertext on reading ability was reported in this study.

Megarry (1991) has described another interesting hypermedia project called 'Europe in the Round' that is devoted to study and work in Europe. The intention of this project was to combine hypertext and mass storage in order to produce a 'powerful learning tool'. Essentially, the product functions as an interactive information system that can provide various types of data about the Member States of the European Community. The original system was developed using HyperCard (for delivery on a Macintosh computer) and was distributed on compact disc (CD-ROM). A version of the system is now also available in ToolBook for IBM PC microcomputers. Figure 4.2 shows some typical examples of the 10,000 screens of which this system is composed.

There is a plethora of interesting descriptions of hypermedia projects conducted in higher education environments. Most of the early development work on educational uses of hypertext and hypermedia was conducted in American universities such as Brown, Cornell, Harvard and the University of Maryland. Subsequently, many interesting European projects were initiated both in the UK and in other EC countries. Typical examples of these include: the StrathTutor system developed at Strathclyde University (Mayes *et al.*, 1988) – this system is discussed in more detail later; the CALSA project at the University of Teesside (Ingraham and Emery, 1991); the Microcosm system at the University of Southampton (Hall, 1993) – this is essentially a 'polymedia' information management system; and the 'Hypermedia for Teaching' project at the University of Barcelona (Barker, 1993a). These are just a few examples of the many different academic projects that are currently underway within the EC.

Hypermedia techniques have been employed in virtually all subject areas within university teaching, ranging from mathematics (Bell *et al.*, 1990); computer science (Smeaton, 1991) and medicine (Kidd *et al*, 1992; Paterson and Adamson, 1992; Whiton *et al.*, 1992) to English (Landlow, 1989a) and law (Gibbons, 1992). A useful general guide to hypertext and hypermedia developments in some of the UK universities recently appeared in *The CTISS File* (CTISS, 1990). A more detailed coverage of the use of hypermedia in the humanities has also been presented by Deegan *et al.*, (1992).

Undoubtedly, some of the most interesting and exciting hypermedia products for educational use are those that are now starting to appear commercially for use in schools, colleges and in the home environment. These are published on compact disc (CD-ROM) for use with a suitable delivery platform (such as CD-I or

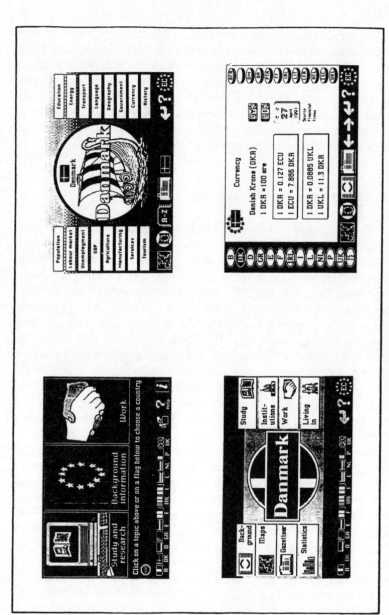

Figure 4.2 Hypermedia in education – 'Europe in the Round'

CDTV). Examples of these products include the various 'Sesame Street' productions for teaching numbers and letters, based upon the use of interactive stories and microworlds that children can explore; the 'Mother Goose' productions – these are electronic activity books; the Discis 'talking books'; and 'Story Machine', a hypermedia system for interactively composing multimedia stories containing pictures, text and sound. Some of these publications are discussed in more detail later in this chapter and in the following one.

Hypermedia in the workplace

For the discussion that follows, the term 'workplace' is used to refer to any location (other than an academic organization) in which people are purposefully engaged in producing consumer products or providing services of some sort. The workplace therefore has a substantial diversity, ranging from factory production lines through to shops, libraries, hospitals, museums, art galleries, railway stations and airports. Examples of hypermedia applications in each of these areas are well-documented in the literature.

In the context of education and training, the ways in which hypermedia is used in the workplace will not be significantly different from the ways in which it is used in academic environments. Indeed, as can be seen from Table 4.1, many of the functional roles of hypertext/hypermedia in the workplace are quite similar.

Broadly, there are two major educational aspects of hypermedia use within a workplace situation. First, its use for internal purposes within an organization for staff training, the induction of new staff and general current awareness using a multi-level approach (this is discussed in more detail below). Second, its use as an educational and promotional resource with respect to the customers of an organization's services and/or products. Because of the importance of customer education, it is now commonplace within many commercial settings to employ hypermedia techniques to develop non-linear point-of-sale information systems for use in stores and various other public places. Some of the earliest applications of hypertext were for the creation of customer-orientated information services for use in museums and art galleries (Baird, 1990; Morrall,

Table 4.1 *Business and commercial uses of hypermedia*

computer system and software documentation
on-line help facilities
creation of dictionaries and encyclopaedias
laws, regulations, standards and guidelines
maintenance manuals
education and training
software design and development
collaborative authoring and research
legal and accounting document management
archival publications
catalogues and databases
public access information systems
advertising and publicity brochures
'info-tainment' and 'edu-tainment'

1991). Hypermedia-based information services for customers are now being provided increasingly within shops, large departmental stores, shopping complexes and hotels.

Two very important training developments in which hypermedia techniques have been figuring quite prominently are the creation of electronic performance support systems (Gery, 1991); and the augmentation of conventional CBT methods in order to improve their effectiveness and flexibility (Richards and Barker, 1993; Subramanian and Jambukesan, 1991).

According to Banerji (1993), an electronic performance support system (EPSS) is:

> a human activity system that is able to manipulate large amounts of task related information in order to provide both a problem solving capability and learning opportunities to augment human performance in a job task by providing information and concepts in a non-linear way, as and when they are required by a user.

In our research (Barker and Banerji, 1993a; 1993b) we have found, in agreement with many other developers, that the EPSS approach is capable of providing a very powerful mechanism for performing on-the-job training using a 'just-in-time' paradigm. Because of the future importance of hypermedia performance support systems for use in workplace education and training we shall discuss this topic further in Chapter 6.

In order to overcome some of the limitations of conventional CBT, Richards and Barker (1993) have described an approach to CBT augmentation based upon the use of hypermedia. Their approach involves combining the attractive features of CBT with the non-linear facilities inherent in the use of hypermedia. They claim that their methodology is able to make CBT much more adaptable and flexible while at the same time making it more interesting by giving the user greater control over the way in which information is accessed and presented.

Fundamental to achieving greater flexibility in a training situation through the use of hypermedia is the ability to create a knowledge corpus that is able to support multiple parallel pathways through it. Each pathway is normally associated with a particular organizational function, for example, a management role, technician support, sales staff, and so on. This idea is illustrated schematically in Figure 4.3.

In this diagram the knowledge corpus provides multiple trails through the hypermedia knowledge corpus. Depending upon how the system is designed, users may be restricted to the particular trail relating to their job function or may be free to switch from one trail

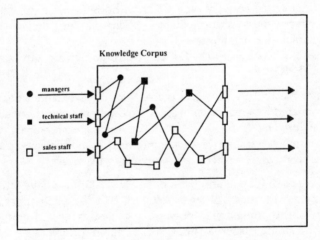

Figure 4.3 *A multi-level hypermedia knowledge corpus*

to another as the need arises. A number of commercial organizations have produced hypermedia training packages of this sort. Unfortunately, the problem with this approach is the substantial amount of design and development activity that is needed in order to implement it successfully. However, once a system of this type has been created it can prove very successful in terms of usability.

Currently, access to hypermedia resources in workplace situations is most often provided through some form of conventional computer system. However, where customers are involved in accessing material, purpose built, easy-to-use access stations often have to be constructed. Increasingly, many consumer products are becoming available which can provide access to hypermedia resources for education and training (some of these are briefly discussed in the following section). Because of their availability these products are also starting to be used for hypermedia access in the workplace. One interesting educational product that is briefly described in the following section is the management training package, 'The Complete Manager', that has recently been released as a CD-I title.

Hypermedia in the home

As was the case in the workplace situation, there are two basic ways of providing access to hypermedia resources in a home environment: through the use of conventional home computer systems and by means of the various consumer products that are now starting to become commercially available. In this section we shall concentrate on the latter approach. Three typical examples of consumer products for use in a home environment will be considered: Commodore's Dynamic Total Vision (CDTV) system; Philips' Compact Disc-Interactive (CD-I); and the Sony Data Discman. The first two of these delivery platforms use a conventional TV set for the display of information. The presentation of hypermedia resources using these will therefore not differ too greatly from those employed in a conventional, but interactive, television. The Data Discman, however, uses a small, backlit liquid crystal display measuring only 6.7 × 5.6 cm. This allows the display of 10 lines of text, each of which can contain up to 30 characters, and a graphics resolution of 256 (horizontal) × 200 (vertical) pixels. The relatively small size of the screen, its limited resolution and monochrome nature will strongly influence the characteristics of the information that can be displayed and, consequently, how hypermedia is designed and delivered.

The Sony Data Discman is an example of a hand-held electronic book delivery platform. Currently, there are many hypermedia electronic books available for use with it, such as 'The Oxford Dictionary and Oxford Thesaurus', 'The Chambers Encyclopedia of Science and Technology' and 'The Hutchinson Guide to the World'. This system is described in more detail in the following chapter.

The Commodore CDTV system and the Philips' CD-I delivery platform are very similar to each other in terms of physical appearance, mode of operation and the functions that are provided. One advantage of the CDTV system is the ease with which it can be upgraded into a fully-fledged home computer system, should the need or desire arise. However, unlike CDTV, CD-I has an advantage in that it is based upon an internationally agreed standard. Unfortunately, although there is much similarity between these two systems, the compact discs that they use are of a different format and so interchange of products between them is not possible.

The basic arrangement of a typical CD-I delivery platform is illustrated schematically in Figure 4.4 (Barker, 1993b). The CD-I unit itself consists of a single 'black box' which is connected to an ordinary television set by means of a single cable. If so desired (for example, to obtain stereo sound) the CD-I unit can also be connected to a hi-fi amplification system. In order to transfer material to video tape, a set of video cassette recorder output connections are also available.

An important component of a CD-I system is its interaction devices. These allow the position of an on-screen cursor to be controlled. Typical interaction devices include the thumb-stick controller; the CD-I mouse; and the roller-controller (Philips IMS, 1992). In Figure 4.4 the use of the roller-controller is illustrated; it consists of two basic components: a central roller-ball that can be rotated in any direction and a set of two action buttons (B1 and B2). The roller-controller is used to position the screen cursor over a

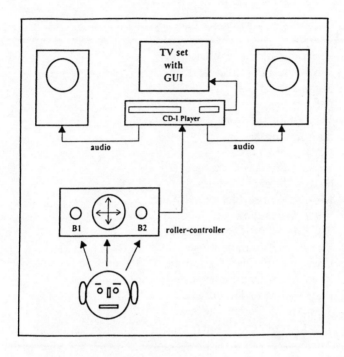

Figure 4.4 *Schematic arrangement of Philips' CD-I equipment*

displayed object, then one or other of the action buttons is pressed in order to select and/or activate the object of interest. One very obvious advantage of the CD-I system, both for home users and for non-technically orientated people is its simplicity and ease of use.

A range of CD products based on conventional and hypermedia design are available for use with the CD-I delivery platform in a home (or classroom or work) environment. Some of the currently available titles are listed in Table 4.2.

'Treasures of the Smithsonian' implements a museum metaphor that gives users the impression that they are entering a museum and walking around exploring the exhibits in the way that they choose. A variety of ways of accessing exhibits is provided – via a time-line, alphabetical reference list, subject category, guided tour and so on. Each exhibit in the museum is illustrated by one or more photographs and described using a high-quality audio narration;

119

Table 4.2 *Examples of CD-I titles*

Treasures of the Smithsonian
Time Life Photography
Stamps
Mozart
Harvest of the Sun: Van Gogh
Sargon Chess
Great British Golf
Sesame Street – Numbers
Sesame Street – Letters
Mother Goose Nursery Rhymes
Cartoon Jukebox
Tell Me Why (Discs I and II)
The French Impressionists
Create Your Own Caricature
Rand McNally's America
Renaissance of Florence
The Art of Dutch Masters
The Complete Manager

sound effects are also used where they are appropriate. For many exhibits, extra information is available if the user wishes to access it. The information for a given exhibit is hyper-linked to other exhibits where this is appropriate. Control of the presentation of material is always in the hands of the user; at any instant, information presentation can be paused, resumed, repeated or exited, depending upon what a particular user wishes to do.

The Time Life '35 mm Photography' disc is essentially a multimedia, interactive, user-controlled tutorial. Its intent is to teach people how to improve their photographic skills. During the tutorial, users can exercise and test their skills using the various camera simulations that are built into the disc. This particular product is interesting in that it is one of the few that use partial-screen motion video to good effect.

Undoubtedly, there is a growing number of delivery environments (and products to run on them) starting to become available for use in home environments. Often, these are referred to as 'info-tainment' or 'edu-tainment' products because they attempt to combine an educational experience with one which is also entertaining. In many ways this is a major step forward in the relatively low-cost availability of interactive educational resources for use in home environments, especially if it can be shown to be pedagogically effective.

Case studies

This section briefly describes three case studies involving the development of hypermedia systems for educational use. The first of these outlines the basic facilities provided by an authoring and delivery environment (called 'StrathTutor') for presenting on-line tutorials in a university setting. The second case study is concerned with the design of a multi-lingual hypermedia teaching package for use within the EC, called 'Hypermedia for Teaching'. The third case study, on 'Euro-Publisher', describes how hypermedia methods are currently being employed in software products in order to improve their quality, accessibility and learnability.

StrathTutor

StrathTutor is a learning-by-browsing tutorial system that was developed some years ago by the University of Strathclyde in the UK. The original intent of the system was 'to deliver Bioscience teaching to first year University students' using Apple Macintosh computers. The overall system contains three basic units: a delivery tool; an authoring tool; and a trace facility. The system was programmed primarily in Microsoft BASIC with some time-critical sections being coded in assembly language. Students interact with StrathTutor solely by means of a mouse. Considerable attention was given to the design of the system's human–computer interface which was based upon the standard WIMP (windows-icon-mouse-pointer) interface associated with Apple Macintosh computers.

The StrathTutor system is described by its authors as a 'content free tutorial shell within which CAL browsing tutorials can be produced' (Mayes *et al.*, 1988). Tutorials for delivery by StrathTutor are created using the authoring tool, called 'STmaker'. The trace facility, known as 'STviewer', enables a learner's interaction with and pathway through a tutorial to be monitored and recorded. The trace that is made can subsequently be played back and analysed for research purposes. STviewer is essentially a research tool.

One of the most attractive features of the StrathTutor system, according to its authors, is its ease of use: 'both the delivery system and the authoring system are fully usable after a few minutes of explanation'. Essentially, the STmaker authoring system organizes knowledge into screen-based frames. Within these frames text and graphics can be entered with equal facility. Also, frames that have been designed using standard Macintosh text and graphics tools can be easily incorporated into a tutorial file. Each frame in a tutorial is coded by its author using a system of attributes; up to 60 attributes may be named. A picture can be coded by attributes in exactly the same way as a piece of text. During the authoring process an author of a tutorial can also use a mouse in order to designate rectangular hotspots of any size on the screen of the computer and code each of these with a selection of attributes. Overall, the attributes that are used in a tutorial form a knowledge base in which a subset of its author's expertise is embedded.

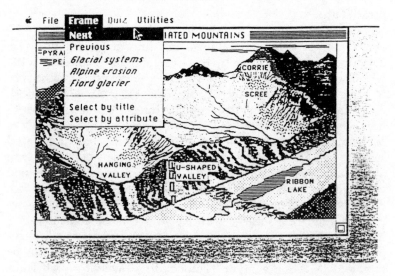

Figure 4.5 *StrathTutor screen showing the contents of the 'frame' menu*

Students interact with StrathTutor using screens similar to that shown in Figure 4.5. Four main menu options are available. 'File' provides access to help, facilities for starting and joining tutorials, printing frames and leaving the system. As can be seen from the figure, the 'Frame' menu allows access to other frames using a number of different strategies: 'Next' is the default and chooses the closest frame (see below) and 'Previous' allows for back-tracking. The three 'named' frames are selected algorithmically based upon a process of frame attribute matching. 'Select by title' allows a learner to browse through the titles of all frames in the current tutorial while 'Select by attribute' allows learners to interrogate the knowledge base in a way that is similar to querying a database. Users can also click on hotspots within a displayed frame. Again, the proximity algorithm is used to retrieve the frame which is the best match to the attribute configuration associated with the selected hotspots.

During their interaction with a tutorial, students can undertake a quiz in order to assess how well they are progressing. This is designed in the form of a game with the allocation of 'game points' depending upon the quality of the answers given by the student. At any given time while they are using the system students can also ask why particular frames have been shown, using the 'Utilities' menu.

StrathTutor offers a very useful approach to learning-by-browsing since students are given many different opportunities for concept learning. However, the system has been criticized for its lack of scope for providing guidance. In response, the authors claim that this limitation could be easily overcome by redefining frames as sequences of screens that are presented in a fixed order.

'Hypermedia for Teaching'

'Hypermedia for Teaching' is a multinational development project that is sponsored by the Commission of the European Communities under its COMETT research and development programme. The project involves partners from each of the member states of the EC. The objective of the project is to produce a multi-lingual teaching and awareness package that describes hypermedia and its potential as a learning and training resource (Barker, 1993a). The material that makes up the training package is to be published as an interactive compact disc (CD-ROM) in the first instance, for use within an IBM PC environment, and will later be published in CD-I format for delivery using Philips' CD-I players. For the first CD-ROM production the Asymetrix ToolBook system is being used as the authoring environment. Multi-lingual audio narrations will be generated from digitally recorded sound using a SOUND BLASTER card that is embedded within the PC-based delivery station.

The pedagogic material that makes up the basic package is organized into a series of relatively independent modules. The modules themselves fall into one of two distinct categories: the 'common core' (CC) modules and the 'application' (AP) modules. The relationship between these modules is illustrated schematically in Figure 4.6A and the titles of the individual modules are listed in Table 4.3.

Table 4.3 *Component modules of 'Hypermedia for Teaching'*

CC1	Introduction
CC2	Basic Concepts
CC3	History of Hypertext
CC4	Creation of Hypertext
CC5	Navigation
CC6	Hypermedia
AP1	Higher Education
AP2	Company Training
AP3	Foreign Language Learning
AP4	Project Management
AP5	Banking

In the original specification of the system it was intended that a multi-level approach should be used, similar to that illustrated in Figure 4.3. Six basic levels were initially identified as being important from the point of view of the target audience for which the product was intended. The target audience was computer-literate users who had little or no experience with hypermedia. The

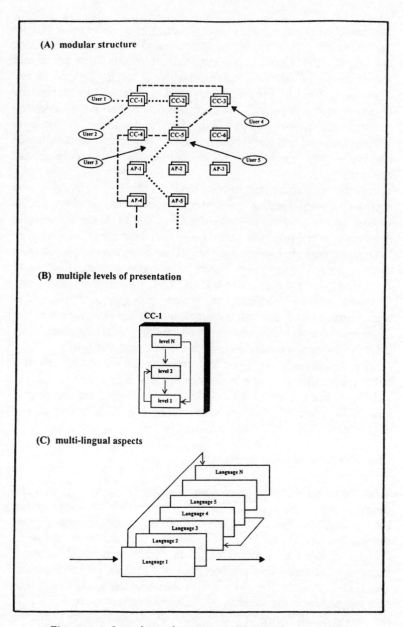

Figure 4.6 *Some design dimensions in 'Hypermedia for Teaching'*

particular level at which a user entered the system was to be calculated on the basis of a simple pre-test about hypermedia. Once an initial level had been assigned, individual users would subsequently be allowed to transfer to other levels (see Figure 4.6B) as and when they felt the need. Unfortunately, when the resource implications for implementing this design were calculated it was found that it would not be feasible to adopt a multi-level approach as had originally been hoped. Consequently, a redesign of the system was undertaken so as to implement a 'middle-person' approach.

Another important design consideration that had to be taken into account when designing the system was the way in which multi-lingual access was to be provided. The contract for the project required that the product should be accessible through six European languages; English, French, Spanish, Italian, German and Dutch were chosen. As can be seen from Figure 4.6C it was intended that at any particular instant a user could switch from one language to another. However, due to 'continuity' problems, arising from differences in the languages, and resource implications, this did not prove feasible. Therefore, it was only possible to allow users to change languages prior to entering or after leaving a module, but not within it.

The 'Hypermedia for Teaching' project is an interesting one due to its multinational nature and its substantial scope. The CD-ROM version of the product is well on its way to completion and once it has been evaluated the production of the CD-I version will commence.

The 'Euro-Publisher' Project

'Euro-Publisher' forms part of a much larger European research and development project called 'ILDIC' – Integrating Learning Design into Interactive Compact Disc. ILDIC is a multinational project funded by the Council for the European Communities as part of its DELTA research initiative (DELTA is an acronym for Developing European Learning through Technological Advance). The intent of the ILDIC project was to explore how to design learning and training products for subsequent delivery from interactive compact disc. The ILDIC project went through several distinct phases: evaluation of existing products using 'competitive analysis'; the formulation of a model for learning design; testing and evaluation of the model through the creation of prototypes; and the subsequent evaluation of the prototypes themselves.

During the ILDIC project four basic prototypes were created and published on interactive CD. One of these prototypes involved producing a hypermedia 'electronic manual' for an existing software product known as 'Timeworks Publisher'. Timeworks is a desktop publishing (DTP) package that runs on IBM PC computers within the environment provided by the Microsoft Windows graphical user interface. Currently, Timeworks is distributed to purchasers in a large cardboard box that contains several floppy discs and a paper-based manual. The system is available in several European languages (English, French, German and Spanish) and versions for the other European languages are being produced.

The purpose of producing a hypermedia electronic reference manual for the Timeworks system was twofold: first, to see how the availability of such a manual might necessitate the redesign of the overall system; second, to see how publishing everything on an optical medium might overcome some of the problems the company faced as a result of having to distribute a polymedia product (software on floppy disc and reference manual on paper) in several different languages. It was thought that the use of an electronic manual would improve the product from both the producer's and the users' points of view. For example, by distributing the overall system on compact disc it was thought that it would be possible to provide additional features and capabilities that could not be supported by manuals published in paper form.

The overall design of the system, as it currently stands, is illustrated schematically in Figure 4.7. The tutorial system is intended to provide basic instruction, in an interactive fashion, about the Timeworks DTP package. While in tutorial mode, users can access Timeworks and try things out. They can also use the help facility and the hypermedia reference manual. However, established users, who are actually involved in using the Timeworks package to create a publication, will primarily only need to access the electronic manual to look up things of which they are not sure. The functional specification of the hypermedia reference manual is outlined in Table 4.4.

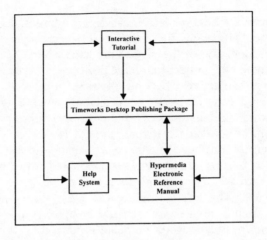

Figure 4.7 *Re-designed publishing package (Euro-Publisher)*

Table 4.4 *Functional requirements of the hypermedia manual*

- access to different topics using a hyperlinking method
- provision of an index
- a glossary should be available
- full-text searching is allowed
- ability to print out a particular topic or section
- a meta-help system must be available
- table of contents to be provided
- access to the Timeworks Publisher program
- provision for making annotations
- addition of bookmarks
- keyword explanations
- a history function should be available
- navigation facilities must be provided

The prototype hypermedia reference manual has been published on CD-ROM and integrated into the DTP package. Some quite novel features of the electronic version of the manual include the use of audio narration for the presentation of summary material and general guidance, and the use of two extra interactive features – 'show me' and 'practice'. The 'show me' command is essentially a concise demonstration facility which, when invoked, will show users how to perform a particular task such as indentation, italicization, cut and paste and so on. The 'practice' facility allows users to practise particular skills or features before actually applying them to real data.

In the example described in this case study the use of hypermedia techniques in conjunction with CD-ROM publication has provided benefits for both the users of the software and its producers. For users, the new system provides easier access to a wider range of interactive features while for the manufacturer the product has become both easier to handle and to distribute.

Conclusion

This chapter has considered some existing and potential roles for hypermedia within the context of an educational and training framework. Obviously, many important factors have to be considered if the technique is to be used successfully to support learning activities. Some of these factors have been identified and discussed within this chapter.

Two major advantages associated with the use of the hypermedia technique are greater pedagogic freedom for the user and greater flexibility for the designer of educational resources. In giving users greater freedom to explore and control a hypermedia knowledge corpus, it is important to ensure that they do not 'misuse' their power and become lost, confused or overwhelmed with information. The use of suitable metaphors can help to minimize the effects of this problem.

We have shown in this chapter that hypermedia can be used to support learning and training activities in a variety of different contexts and situations: within the classroom, the workplace and the home. Because there are many different ways of using this technique there is an increasing demand for hypermedia resources for teaching and training purposes by both teachers and students.

In the following chapter we shall discuss an important mechanism for providing access to hypermedia resources. The mechanism that we shall adopt will be based upon a book metaphor.

5 Hypermedia Electronic Books

Introduction

Before the advent of television, film, radio and computer systems, books were the most important method of documenting, storing and disseminating knowledge in a reliable way. Although conventional books published on paper are still very important, they do suffer from a number of serious limitations (Barker, 1992c). In view of this, some years ago we made a detailed analysis of the role of conventional books in technical knowledge dissemination processes (Barker and Manji, 1988). We identified a number of important shortcomings of such books (see Table 5.1) and suggested that some new form of book was needed in order to overcome the limitations of those which are published on paper.

We used the term 'electronic book' to describe a new form of book whose pages were composed, not of static printer's ink, but from dynamic electronic information. Generally, we now use this new term to describe information delivery systems that are capable of providing their users with access to pages of reactive electronic information with which they can interact. As we shall discuss in the following section, the pages of information which make up an electronic book are organized conceptually just like the pages of a conventional book.

The properties of a book will depend critically upon the medium upon which it is published. Nowadays, five basic media are commonly used for this purpose: paper, microfilm, electronic mass storage, magnetic disc and optical disc. Unfortunately, publication on paper or microfilm renders the information embedded in a book

Table 5.1 *Basic limitations of conventional books*

- difficult to reproduce (reprographically)
- expensive to disseminate
- difficult to update
- single copies cannot easily be shared
- easily damaged and vandalized
- bulky to transport
- embedded material is unreactive and static
- cannot utilize sound
- cannot utilize animation or moving pictures
- unable to monitor reader's activity
- cannot assess reader's understanding
- unable to adapt material dynamically
- most books are essentially linear in nature
- supports 'telling' rather than 'constructing'

static and unreactive. In order to make its information reactive and dynamic the book concerned must be published on a suitable 'interactive medium' (Barker, 1991a). Most electronic books will therefore be published on electronic, magnetic or digital optical storage media. Although books published on electronic and magnetic media are useful, they are not as useful as those that are produced using optical storage. The substantial utility of optical media arises from their large storage capacity, robustness and relative cheapness. Two types of optical storage media are commonly used for producing electronic books: magneto-optical rewritable disc storage (Roth, 1991) and compact disc read-only-memory (CD-ROM) (Lambert and Ropiequet, 1986).

Although a considerable amount of work is undertaken using rewritable optical disc (mainly for testing and prototyping purposes), the optical medium that is most often used for electronic book publication is CD-ROM. As well as its durability and stability, the other attractive feature of CD-ROM as a publication medium for electronic books is its immense storage capacity. A single CD-ROM is able to store a total of 650 Mbytes of information. In terms of the magnetic storage available on a low-capacity 5.25 inch floppy disc, this is equivalent to about 1800 floppy discs!

The 650 Mbytes of storage available with a CD-ROM disc can be used in a variety of different ways for the storage of multimedia information such as text, sound, static pictures, animation, computer programs and a very limited amount of motion video. Typical figures that are often quoted to reflect the storage capacity of a CD-ROM disc are: 200,000 pages of A4 text; or 20,000 low-quality (PCX) image files; or 2,000 TV quality still images; or 30 seconds of video; or 18 hours of low-quality sound. The way in which the available storage is used within a given electronic book production will depend critically on the media mix needed by the particular publication concerned.

The actual amount of material that can be stored on a CD-ROM disc will depend upon whether or not any form of data compression technique is applied to the information before it is committed to storage. Normally, in order to store full-motion video pictures on a CD-ROM, various types of compression and decompression techniques must be applied.

From the point of view of electronic book publication, the most commonly used CD-ROM format is that specified in the ISO 9660 standard. This is an internationally recognized way of storing information on a CD-ROM so that it can be read by any computer system that has a suitable disc drive attached to it. Unfortunately, the ISO 9660 standard does impose some restrictions on what can be done with a CD-ROM disc. In order to overcome these restrictions, several other approaches to using CD-ROM are rapidly emerging. The four most important of these are: CD-ROM XA (extended architecture); CD-I (compact disc interactive); CDTV (Commodore's Dynamic Total Vision); and DVI (Digital Video Interactive). Each of these offers many exciting possibilities for the design of electronic books.

For a variety of reasons, electronic books are rapidly becoming an important pedagogic resource. Because of their importance in the context of learning and training activity, the remainder of this chapter discusses a number of issues relating to their production and use. We shall first discuss their basic architecture and some of the important factors that need to be considered during their design and fabrication. A taxonomic framework which enables books of this sort to be classified will then be presented. The special features of hypermedia electronic books will then be discussed. Finally, some examples of different types of hypermedia electronic book will be briefly presented.

Delivery platforms

Unlike conventional books, those that are published on electronic media require some form of 'delivery platform' to facilitate access to them. Unfortunately, although a large number of electronic books exist, there seems to be no 'standard' delivery platform that will enable all the currently available electronic books to be accessed. Each particular type of electronic book that is presently available seems to need its own specific tailor-made delivery platform. Three examples will be used to illustrate this point.

Consider first the 'expanded books' produced by the Voyager Company for delivery platforms based upon suitably configured Apple Macintosh computers. 'Jurassic Park' (Crichton, 1991) is just one example of the many electronic book titles that have recently been released by this company. Each one consists of a single 3.5 inch magnetic disc containing compressed multimedia information that must be loaded onto a hard disc before it can be accessed. Once the contents of the disc have been installed, the electronic text and diagrams provide a 'dynamic medium' that enables a user to 'become a more active reader'.

As a second example consider the electronic books that have been produced for delivery on the Sony Data Discman electronic book player (Rockman, 1992). Hutchinson's 'Guide to the World' (Helicon Publishing, 1992) is a typical example of a publication that has been produced for delivery using this platform. Each of the available publications consists of a single 8 cm digital optical storage disc (of the read-only variety) embedded within a caddy that makes its appearance very similar to the expanded books that were described above. Although similar in appearance, these books are totally incompatible with those intended for the Macintosh or any other currently available delivery platform.

The third example is taken from an electronic book series being produced by the Elsevier publishing company – known as the 'Active Library' series. A typical publication in this series is the 'Active Library on Corrosion' (Bogaerts and Agema, 1992), published on a 12 cm CD-ROM disc for delivery using an IBM PC platform that is equipped with the Microsoft Windows 3.1 graphical user interface. Again, this electronic publication (and its host delivery platform) is totally incompatible with either of the other two products that have been previously mentioned.

Despite the gloomy incompatibility problems outlined above, some rationale is starting to emerge with respect to electronic book architectures, along two different basic directions; first, in terms of the fundamental structure and composition of delivery platforms; and second, in terms of how users are meant to perceive the conceptual structure of an electronic book publication.

The basic architecture and composition of a typical electronic book delivery platform is illustrated schematically in Figure 5.1. Four basic components are needed: either an embedded or an explicit computer facility (for control purposes and in order to achieve overall system integration); a multimedia information

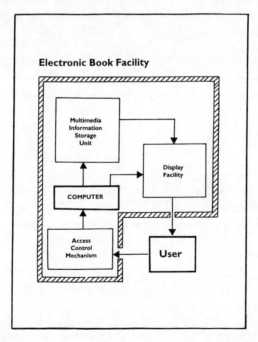

Figure 5.1 *Basic structure of an electronic book delivery station*

storage device (such as a CD-ROM unit); a display facility that enables users to see (and/or hear) the information contained in an electronic book; and a suitable access control mechanism. This latter component will usually consist of a suitably designed hardware interface (such as a keyboard and mouse) and a software environment to control the retrieval and presentation of information. The nature of electronic book software varies considerably and can be used in many different ways to influence how users will perceive a particular publication.

Figure 5.2 shows how the schematic electronic book architecture described above can be realized through the use of a multimedia personal computer (MPC). The MPC provides an example of a polyfunctional workstation that embeds a CD-ROM drive and a sound-card (for generating audio from digital sound files). The MPC configuration illustrated in Figure 5.2 also contains a modem card to enable the electronic book workstation to be connected to a telephone network, and hence, other computers, electronic libraries, cyberspaces and telemedia books (these items are explained later in the chapter).

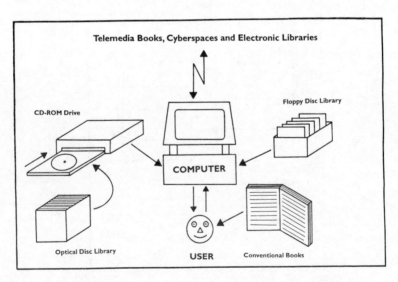

Figure 5.2 *Polyfunctional workstation for electronic book delivery*

136

In order to understand how computers can be used to implement electronic books it is important to have an appropriate conceptual view of this type of publication. One useful conceptual model that now underlies the development of many electronic book publications is illustrated schematically in Figure 5.3. This depicts an electronic book in terms of a collection of reactive and dynamic pages of multimedia information, that can embed text, pictures and sound. The information contained within these pages is of three basic types: aesthetic (which, through its appearance, is used both to help reinforce the underlying book metaphor and also to provide an ergonomically 'pleasing' effect); informative (which is intended to instruct or inform those who use a particular book); and either implicit or explicit control functions. The control options that are available are important because they enable users to specify the nature of the information that they wish to retrieve from a given

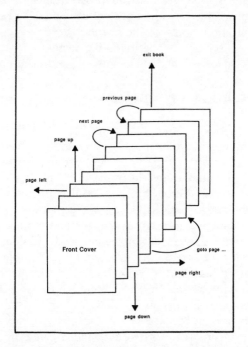

Figure 5.3 *Conceptual model for electronic book production*

137

book and how this retrieved material is to be displayed within the confines of the host delivery platform. Some examples of simple primitive control options for electronic books are illustrated in Figure 5.3. The most commonly used functions are: next page; previous page; goto page N; exit book and so on.

The basic control options that are used within the pages of an electronic book may take the form of icons, dynamic menus, dialogue boxes, scroll bars and/or hotspots. The reactive areas that make up hotspots may be embedded within chunks of screen-based text and/or pictures (these form the basis of the 'hypermedia' electronic books that we discuss later). The particular combination of control options made available within any given publication will depend on a variety of factors, such as the type of book involved; the purpose for which it is intended; the logical and physical sizes of its pages; whether it has a linear or non-linear structure and so on.

When designing and producing an electronic book it is important to give ample consideration to all those design factors that are likely to influence the overall impact, effectiveness and efficiency of the final publication. Some of the factors that we have found to be important are discussed in the following section.

Electronic book production

The design, fabrication and dissemination of electronic books is rapidly becoming a major area of activity within both education and the publishing industry. Some years ago, because of the importance of this topic we initiated an 'electronic book' project. This project, which commenced in 1990 (Barker and Giller, 1992a), was intended to explore the use of CD-ROM for the publication of electronic books. Three particular objectives that we had in mind were: a) to try and formulate a set of design guidelines to facilitate electronic book production, paying particular attention to the role of end-user interfaces; b) to assess the potential of electronic books as a mechanism for the distribution of interactive training and learning resources for use in distance education and flexible learning environments; and c) to explore the use of hypermedia electronic books as a means of structuring and navigating non-linear multimedia knowledge corpora.

During our project two basic research and development strands were pursued. The first of these involved an evaluative study of a range of commercially available electronic book publications – such as 'The New Grolier Encyclopedia (Grolier, 1988) and Compton's Multimedia Encyclopedia (Britannica Software, 1990; 1991). The second strand involved the design, production and controlled evaluation of a number of in-house productions. Three different in-house electronic book demonstrators were produced (Giller, 1992). These provided examples of a hypermedia book entitled 'An Electronic Book for Early Learners'; a multimedia book entitled 'Screen Design for Computer-based Training'; and an intelligent electronic book called 'A Static Picture Book with Audio Narrations'. Each demonstrator was designed to explore a different aspect of electronic book production.

In our research project we discovered that two basic types of design tool were needed to facilitate the creation of electronic books. The first of these was a set of high-level design models while the second constituted a collection of more pragmatic low-level 'tips' (or guidelines) relating to end-user interface design; the way information is organized on CD-ROM; and the effective creation of access stations for use with electronic books.

The most important of our findings was the set of three high-level development models that we formulated. We refer to these as the 'conceptual' model (shown in Figure 5.3), the 'design' model and the 'fabrication' model. The first of these is intended for end-users of electronic books as an orientation tool. The second and third models are intended for designers and producers of electronic books as they describe architectural and procedural issues, respectively.

When designing electronic books we found that the basic design model shown in Figure 5.4 was an extremely useful asset (Barker, 1990; Barker and Manji, 1990; Giller, 1992). A major objective of the initial design phase of an electronic book is the formulation of the end-user interfaces that will be used to enable users to access the information that is held within it (Richards, 1993). Book and page structures then have to be decided upon (Barker, 1991b). The content of the book must then be specified. Finally, the nature of the 'reader services' (browsers, bookmarks, glossaries, etc.) must be agreed upon. As can be seen from Figure 5.4, the use of a suitably designed knowledge corpus is fundamental to the creation of our

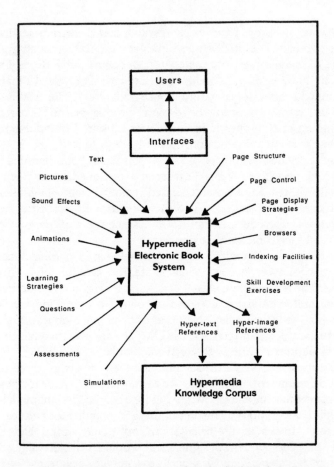

Figure 5.4 *Design model for electronic book production*

electronic books. The attractive feature of CD-ROM as a publication medium is the large capacity that it offers for the storage of multimedia and hypermedia knowledge corpora.

The creation of electronic books requires a number of different development stages. These need to be rigorously adhered to if efficient production is to be achieved. The fabrication model is therefore used to describe the relationships between the various stages that are involved in transferring materials from the initial development phase (based upon the use of hard disc and rewritable optical disc for CD-ROM emulation) through prototyping to the final production stage (using read-only discs). It is these latter discs (in ISO 9660 format) that are distributed to users of our products. The fabrication model that we use to support our electronic book productions is very similar to the general production scheme for developing hypermedia resources that was previously illustrated in Figure 2.6 and described in Chapter 2 in the section on creating hypertext and hypermedia.

As can be seen from this figure, the initial development phase of an electronic book project involves specifying the content and structure of the book. These are then brought together by means of the scripting process. The script gives a detailed specification of the material that is to be embedded within the book (on a page by page basis) and the relationship between the pages, control mechanisms and end-user tools that are to be made available. It will also embed details of all the textual, sonic and pictorial information that is needed for the electronic book pages. The creation of the script will therefore involve the simultaneous production of all the multimedia resources needed for the book. Once these have been created and individually tested the next phase of electronic book production can commence. This will involve integrating and synchronizing the multimedia resources and, in the case of a hypermedia book, interlinking them in appropriate ways.

When the integrating, interlinking and synchronizing phase of electronic book production is complete, the evaluation and testing phases can commence. This may involve the generation of various kinds of 'prototype book'. Once the results of the evaluation and testing have been obtained any final emendations can be incorporated before the final CD-ROM product is mastered, replicated and distributed to users.

During the course of our research into electronic book production we were able to formulate a range of useful design guidelines. We took some trouble to document these as we anticipated that they would be of help to other people who might wish to become involved in electronic book production. The series of guidelines that we produced fell naturally into six basic categories: knowledge engineering; page design; interaction styles; end-user tools and services; use of multimedia; and use of hypermedia. Further detailed descriptions of the guidelines are given elsewhere (Barker and Giller, 1992b; Giller, 1992; Richards, 1993).

Types of electronic book

Electronic books can be classified in a variety of different ways depending upon the medium that they are published on, the functions they perform and the types of facility and service they provide. One very simple taxonomy proposed by Barker and Giller (1992c) categorizes electronic books into four basic classes: archival; informational; instructional; and interrogational.

The first category of book offers a method of storing large volumes of information relating to some particular subject area. Within such books the end-user interface will normally be designed in such a way that it will permit a variety of different methods of information retrieval. Examples of such books include large catalogue systems and databases of records and data, such as 'The New Grolier Encyclopedia' (Grolier, 1988) and 'Compton's Multimedia Encyclopedia' (Britannica Software, 1990; 1991). In many ways, electronic books that fall into the informational category overlap with those in the archival category. However, the stored information is usually less comprehensive and more specific, relating to a particular topic area. An example of this category of electronic book is 'The Oxford Textbook of Medicine on Compact Disc' (Weatherall *et al.*, 1989). The third category of electronic book – instructional – is intended to provide a means of achieving highly efficient and effective skill and knowledge transfer mechanisms for the support of learning and training activities. Users of such books are given the opportunity to learn and progress at their own pace using their own particular style of learning. Some electronic books in this category will actually assess and adapt to their user's personal learning style. Such books automatically reconfigure the material that is presented so as to accommodate its user's preferred approach to learning. Our 'Screen design for computer-based training' (Giller, 1992) is an example of an instructional electronic book. The intention of the last category of electronic book – interrogational – is to support testing, quizzing and assessment activities which will enable readers to gauge their depth of knowledge about a particular topic. This type of book contains three essential components: a question (or exercise) bank; a testing and assessment package; and an expert system. The latter is used to analyse a reader's responses and deduce an appropriate grade or level of competence based on these responses.

Although the taxonomy described above is a useful one, it is often advantageous to use one which is more 'fine-grained'. In view of this requirement, we now propose a taxonomy that contains ten basic classes of electronic book (Barker, 1991a; 1991b) differentiated by the type of information they embed and the kinds of facility they make available:

text books;
static picture books;
moving picture books;
talking books;
multimedia books;
polymedia books;
hypermedia books;
intelligent electronic books;
telemedia electronic books;
and cyberspace books.

Each of these categories of electronic book is briefly discussed below.

As their name suggests, text books are composed of pages of textual material that have been organized into suitably sized chunks of information. The chunk size that is employed will depend upon the screen size that is used for information display and the number of chunks/page that it is required to present simultaneously. Static picture books consist of a collection of pictures that are organized into some particular theme; the pictures may be of various 'qualities' with respect to their resolution and range of colours that they embed. Moving picture books are constructed from either animation clips or motion video segments – or combinations of these; the 'mix' used will depend upon a variety of factors such as the purpose of the electronic book and the 'message' that it is to convey. Talking books depend for their success upon recorded sound (both high- and low-quality) that is used in conjunction with a variety of 'interactive audio' techniques to facilitate end-user control of information and knowledge transfer.

Multimedia books use various combinations of two or more communication channels (either in sequence or simultaneously) in order to encode a particular message. Such books use text, sound, pictures and moving images that are basically organized in a linear fashion. The materials are delivered by means of a single delivery medium (such as magnetic disc or CD-ROM). Polymedia books, in contrast to multimedia books, use a combination of several different media (CD-ROM, magnetic disc, paper and so on) in order to deliver their information to end-users. Hypermedia electronic books have much in common with multimedia books in that they depend upon the use of multiple communication channels. However, unlike multimedia books, hypermedia books employ non-linear organizations of information based upon the use of web-like structures (Barker, 1992d). Because of the embedded intelligence that they contain, intelligent books are in many ways similar to the 'interrogational' books described by Barker and Giller (1992c). These books are capable of dynamic adaptation as a consequence of interaction with end-users. Two of the most exciting types of book that we are currently developing are telemedia books and cyberspace books. The first of these uses telecommunication facilities (see Figure 5.2) to augment the capabilities of a CD-ROM publication in order to support highly interactive distributed distance learning activities (Barker 1992e; 1993c; Barker and Giller, 1992d). Cyberspace books are used as a means of providing their readers with access to various types of virtual reality facility; such books employ different kinds of interactive simulation environment in order to provide end-users with participative, 'real-life' encounters that they would not normally be able to experience.

Because of their importance in the context of promoting independent learning activities, hypermedia electronic books are discussed in more detail in the remainder of this chapter.

Hypermedia electronic books

Earlier, in Figure 5.3, we presented a basic conceptual model for electronic books. This model can be used as a basis for creating many different types of electronic book structure. Obviously, the actual structure that is employed in any given situation will depend primarily on the type of material that the book is to contain and the purpose for which the book is to be used. Most of the simple electronic book structures that we create consist of four basic types of page: a front cover; a contents page; a series of 'root pages'; and a collection of 'target pages'. The relationship between these is illustrated schematically in Figure 5.5 (Barker, 1992a).

Root pages are simply pages that can be reached directly from the contents page of any given book. In many ways they are analogous to 'chapter headers' in conventional books. Target pages are pages that are normally accessed from a parent root node although they could be accessed directly if their individual page numbers or identities are known. They can also be accessed directly by means of an index, if one is available. Depending upon how an

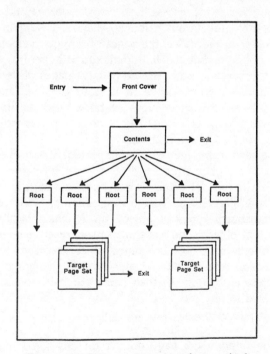

Figure 5.5 *Basic structure of an electronic book*

electronic book is designed, target page clusters can be of two basic types: static and dynamic. Static clusters consist of a fixed collection of given pages whereas dynamic clusters are created as and when they are required according to the particular needs of a given user. Dynamic page structures are particularly important in the case of multimedia and hypermedia electronic books since the media mix used on any given page can significantly influence its commu- nicative and instructional effectiveness.

Multimedia and hypermedia electronic books have much in common but they differ considerably with respect to page reactivity and the way in which their pages are interlinked. Both types of book are based upon the use of pages that can embed text, static pictures, moving pictures and sound resources. However, as has just been mentioned, there is a major difference in the nature of the reactivity of their constituent pages. The reactivity of the pages of a multimedia book arises from three basic sources: page control mechanisms; the need to access local page resources; and the need to gain access to global book resources (Barker, 1992a). In addition to these sources of reactivity, the pages of a hypermedia book will also embed hotspots that enable hypertext and hyperimage links to be followed through to other related reactive pages of information. These additional hotspots serve to identify the real (and major) difference between the two types of book. That is, multimedia books are essentially linear in their mode of presentation while hypermedia books use a non-linear approach.

As can be seen from Figure 5.4, an important aspect of electronic book design is the page structure of its constituent pages (Richards *et al.*, 1991). The basic structure of a hypermedia page is illustrated schematically in Figure 5.6. A page is regarded as being composed of three elementary types of object: those which facilitate page control; context objects; and a spatial array of reactive references to other hypermedia page objects. Control objects correspond to icons and menu items that facilitate page turning, navigation, global resource access and so on. As their name suggests, context objects provide both the physical and the informatic background for the other two types of object that are embedded within a particular page.

All of the hypermedia page objects for any given book exist within a 'common pool'. Within Figures 5.4 and 5.6 this common

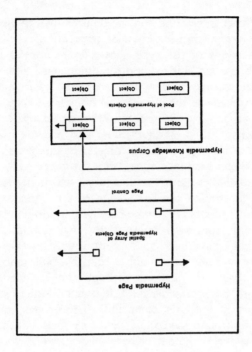

Figure 5.6 *Hypemedia page structure and object pool*

pool is referred to as the 'hypermedia knowledge corpus'. Each object in the pool is identified by means of a unique name. In Figure 5.6 the page references to the supporting hypermedia page objects are denoted by small squares from which arrows emanate. The arrows point to the objects within the common pool which are activated when a user follows up the hypermedia references on any given page. These arrows therefore correspond to hypermedia links. Because objects are in a common pool (which is globally accessible by all pages of the book) there is no need for any duplication of hypermedia objects as a result of different pages requiring to make reference to an identical item.

The structure of the hypermedia objects that are held within the knowledge corpus has been previously illustrated in Figure 3.2C Essentially, all objects have the same binary structure which combines the material to be displayed with the mechanisms for handling end-user interaction and the object's own interaction with other objects held within the knowledge corpus.

From root pages of the type shown in Figure 5.5 users of a hypermedia book can embark upon individualized explorations of the knowledge corpus. As they proceed, the software management system that implements the hypermedia book must keep a record of all the objects that a user references so that a back-track mechanism can be implemented. The system must also provide users with a mechanism for 'marking' particular objects of interest so that they can be recalled and examined again later. A typical exploration path through a knowledge corpus is illustrated schematically in Figure 3.2A. In this illustration the knowledge corpus contains 20 nodes (labelled A to T) of which 10 have been visited. Some of the nodes in the graph structure are labelled with a '@' symbol in order to indicate that they have been 'marked' by the user so that they can be returned to at some later point during the exploration.

To enable users to navigate through the knowledge corpus associated with a hypermedia book it is important to provide an appropriate set of end-user commands. The primary methods of route selection through the corpus will be by means of the hotspots that define the reactive areas of book pages and by means of the standard page control facilities that are provided. However, in order to back-track, a special command will be needed. Similarly, a command will be needed to mark nodes and another will be required to access them (for example, 'mark X' and 'goto X'). A command will also be needed to clear (or unmark) marked nodes when they are of no further immediate interest (for example, 'clear X').

As well as primitive navigation, marking and unmarking commands similar to those described above, a range of other application orientated commands may be required. These will vary from one application to another depending upon the purpose that a particular hypermedia electronic book is to perform. Some examples of different kinds of hypermedia electronic book and the different types of command sets that they use are presented in the following section.

Examples

A number of different hypermedia publications have already been briefly described in previous chapters. In this section some further examples of multimedia and hypermedia electronic books are briefly presented.

The Drexel Electronic Guidebook

One of the earliest attempts to use multimedia and hypermedia techniques within an electronic publication for large scale student use was undertaken by Drexel University in Philadelphia (Hewett, 1987). This electronic guidebook (known as 'The Drexel Disc') was published on magnetic disc. It was designed to run on an Apple Macintosh microcomputer and provided students with a range of different types of information relating to the university and its courses. The basic information categories that are available in the guide are summarized in the 'master menu' illustrated in Figure 5.7A.

Selecting any of the options in this menu leads to another lower-level menu. For example, selecting 'Micro Facilities' leads to the display shown in Figure 5.6B. This menu takes the user closer to the particular interests he or she may have about his or her computer system and its use.

An alternative way of navigating through the disc is by means of the index entry contained in the master menu. Selecting this option takes the reader directly into the 'Drexel Disc Index', a section of which is shown in Figure 5.7C. Users can browse through this, using the scroll bar on the right-hand side of the screen, to find particular items of interest. Once an item has been found, the 'Show' command can be used to go from the index directly to the relevant section of the guide.

Another interesting type of page structure embedded in the Drexel guidebook is illustrated in Figure 5.7D. This is part of the 'Short Cuts and Tips' section of the guide (called 'Apple Jargon'). On the left-hand side of the page is a 'tip selection window', which is scrollable, and on the right-hand side there is a 'tip information window', also scrollable. Selecting a particular item on the left (by double clicking on it) causes its associated information to be

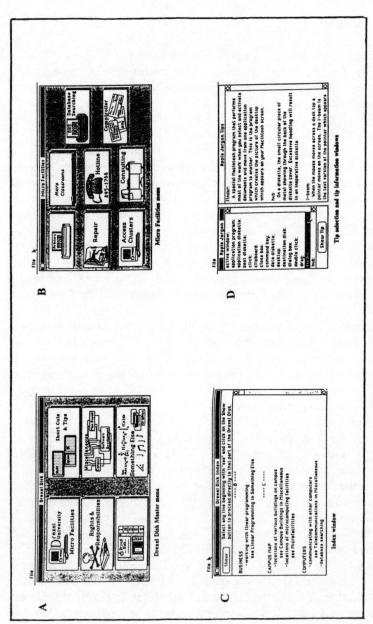

Figure 5.7 *The Drexel Electronic Guide Book*

displayed at the top of the window on the right (in the example shown in Figure 5.7D the user has selected 'finder').

One of the problems of supplying guidebooks such as this to students is the rapidity with which certain types of information go out of date. Quite serious update problems can arise unless an attempt is made to minimize the amount of temporal information contained on the disc.

The Microsoft Bookshelf on CD

Microsoft Bookshelf for Windows is another example of an interactive product in which a book metaphor has been employed. This product, however, is published on compact disc (CD) and runs on a multimedia PC (Jamsa, 1993). Microsoft Bookshelf is an excellent example of the potential that CD-ROM publication can offer for the dissemination of large volumes of information. The single CD contains the equivalent of seven conventional paper-based publications; it provides an atlas, an almanac, a thesaurus, a dictionary, an encyclopaedia and two books of quotations. The particular publications contained on the CD are:

The American Heritage Dictionary
Barrett's Familiar Quotations
The Concise Columbia Dictionary of Quotations
The Concise Columbia Encyclopedia
Hammond Atlas
Roget's II Electronic Thesaurus
The World Almanac and Book of Facts

When the Bookshelf program is installed within the computer each book that it contains is represented on the screen by an icon. The book icons are illustrated in Figure 5.8A – notice how an interactive tutorial is also provided. Double clicking on the Bookshelf icon causes the screen format to change to that illustrated in Figure 5.8B. This shows some of the tools available to support use of the books and navigation through the library and its contents.

Many of the books in the Bookshelf contain high quality pictures (particularly the atlas and the encyclopaedia) which embed reactive areas that facilitate further exploration and navigation. Similarly, many of the text segments contain hypertext links to other related

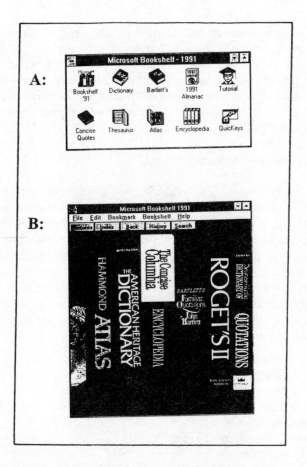

Figure 5.8 *The Microsoft Bookshelf CD*

items of information. Also included on the CD are various animations and sound effects such as quotations, word pronunciations and music.

Electronic books of the type described in this section allow users to retrieve and manipulate information much more easily and quickly than they can with the equivalent paper-based information. There is a growing volume of evidence to support this observation; see, for example, the work by Riding and Chambers (1992) and the evaluations conducted by Landauer *et al.* (1993) in their SuperBook project.

Sony Data Discman publications

The Sony Data Discman is a hand-held portable electronic book delivery platform (Rockman, 1992). It uses 8 cm optical CDs that are normally housed in a caddy that gives them the external appearance of being just like conventional 3.5 inch floppy discs. A range of publications is available for use with this system, including:

The Concise Oxford Dictionary and Thesaurus
Chambers Science and Technology Library
Hutchinson's Guide to the World
Hutchinson's Encyclopedic Dictionary
Harrap's Multilingual Dictionary
The Thomson Electronic Directory
The Electronic Time Out London Guide
Golf Guide Europe

The basic end-user interface to the system consists of a small back-lit LCD and a miniature keyboard containing five function keys, a cursor control pad and yes/no keys. The information contained in most of the electronic books is of a textual nature. However, some books do contain pictorial information; the 'Hutchinson Guide to the World', for example, contains over 500 maps. A variety of search methods is provided to enable information in the books to be accessed. The methods available are based upon: word search; endword search; keyword search; menu search; multi-search; graphics search; and consultation search. Some examples of the 'standard' menu system used for searching are illustrated in Figure 5.9.

Most of the material in the electronic books embeds 'hyperlinks' to related items. For example, by taking the T (thesaurus) entry in screen 4 of Figure 5.9, users can explore the thesaurus entries for the word 'book' and so examine its various meanings such as in 'read a book', 'book a table', and so on. When following through linked information the 'No' key on the keypad allows coarse-grained back-tracking to previous points in the information corpus.

The 'Chambers Science and Technology Library' is in some ways similar to the 'Microsoft BookShelf' described in the previous section since it contains four reference books on one disc:

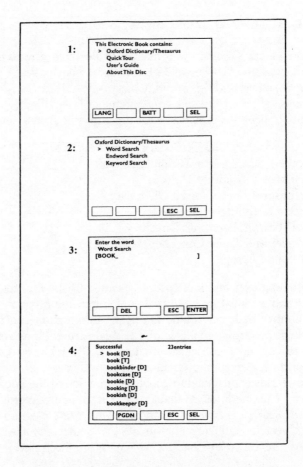

Figure 5.9 *Examples of Sony Data Discman menus*

Science and Technology Dictionary
Great Inventions Through History
Great Modern Inventions
Great Scientific Discoveries

Together, this library contains 45,000 definitions in 50 different subject areas ranging from acoustics to zoology. The disc also contains 650 articles that are interconnected by 13,000 hyperlinks. Although there is a growing number of electronic books becoming available for the Sony Data Discman, few are available specifically for teaching purposes. In view of this deficiency we are currently exploring the potential of hypermedia electronic books for use on this delivery platform (Barker, 1993d).

Elsevier's Active Library series

As we have suggested above, for a variety of reasons, electronic books that are published on compact disc read-only-memory (CD-ROM) are valuable learning resources. Increasingly, publishers are beginning to realize the many advantages of publishing material on CD-ROM for subsequent access using a computer-based delivery platform. The 'Active Library' concept which Elsevier has recently introduced is essentially a generic hypermedia shell into which can be 'plugged' a range of different specialized subject orientated material in order to produce an active library for that subject. The shell itself is written in GUIDE (see Chapters 1 and 3). This is the hypermedia authoring tool that is marketed by Office Workstations Limited (OWL) and which is widely used in many British universities for developing interactive teaching material. Two of the reasons why GUIDE was chosen are the ease with which hypertext links can be created, and its ability to handle SGML – Standard Generalized Markup Language. SGML was used to mark up many of the electronic documents prior to importing them into GUIDE for interlinking using a special tool called GUIDE Writer.

The 'Active Library of Corrosion' (ALC) (Bogaerts and Agema, 1992) is just one of many publications that Elsevier eventually intend to produce as part of their 'Active Library' series. The ALC runs on an IBM PC (or compatibles) within the environment provided by the Windows 3 graphical user interface. It is fairly easy to install from the CD-ROM that it is supplied on and requires about 3.5 MBytes of hard disc space.

Overall, the ALC contains 6000 documents covering a broad range of corrosion topics and comprises:

eight previously published reference works;
1,200 newly created documents written by leading corrosion experts;

over 2,000 images (mostly full colour);
600 formatted tables; and
numerous mathematical and chemical formulae.

Obviously, the system contains a very large amount of information. To give readers a sense of where they are in the publication, the information is organized around the use of a familiar 'library' metaphor. This is designed to provide users with a mental map to use for reference. One screen shows the 'Library Map' with all available sections. Within the individual sections themselves, other maps are provided to aid navigation and to prevent users from getting lost.

The Active Library offers users a range of tools to facilitate working with the electronic knowledge corpus. The functions available include:

specific searches – searching and consulting for information relating to a specific query;
annotations – highlighting and annotating documents or parts of documents;
browsing – reading documents and consulting related documents through links based upon associations; back-tracking is fully supported; and
current awareness – providing up-to-date information on a specific field of interest through a user-profile.

ALC is aimed primarily at individual corrosion engineers. It is intended to serve as a reference work for day-to-day use as well as a source of information on less common corrosion problems. This resource will also be an extremely useful asset within an academic library or laboratory for project work within educational establishments.

Discis Talking Books

The Discis Knowledge Research Corporation in Canada has produced a range of simple hypermedia electronic books on CD-ROM (Discis, 1992). Typical examples of Discis publications include: 'Cinderella', 'The Tale of Benjamin Bunny' and 'The Tale of Peter Rabbit'. Discis books are examples of 'talking' picture story books which are intended for children in the age range 3–9 years.

Each book appears visually on the screen of the computer just like an ordinary book would appear when it is held open for reading. The screen area is divided into two parts, one for the left-hand page and one for the right-hand page of the book being displayed. The pages usually embed high-quality coloured pictures, text and control icons.

An important component of the text pages is the 'loudspeaker' icons which appear on them and which enable the 'talking book' option to be turned on or off. When talking book mode is switched on the text of the story is literally read aloud to the user in English (or a foreign language) with or without automatic page turning. At any point in the story the user can turn audio narration off or stop it temporarily and ask for a repeat pronunciation of a word, phrase or sentence. During the telling of a story various sound effects and musical accompaniments are presented to reinforce the realism and also set up an ambience for its presentation. The sound effects and audio narration are based upon the use of digital audio that is stored on the compact disc upon which the electronic book is published.

One of the attractive features of the Discis books is the way in which it is possible to tailor them to the particular needs of individual users. This is achieved by means of a 'customization' facility which enables a user to specify various 'settings' for the book that is being used. Typical customization parameters include sound and speech volume; language options; the text display parameters to be used (for example, font, size, style, line spacing and so on); and the way in which various tools and icons are to operate.

Discis books are produced to a very high standard, both in terms of the high quality of the sound and graphics and the ability to customize individual products in various ways. In these respects, the quality of Discis publications is currently unrivalled.

Electronic books on CD-I

Some examples of CD-I titles and a description of the delivery platform needed to access these have already been given in Chapter 4 (see Table 4.2 and Figure 4.4). We shall, therefore, conclude this present section of the book by giving short descriptions of two of the currently available CD-I titles that are implemented in the form of simple hypermedia electronic books: the 'Mother Goose' publications and the Smithsonian Institution's 'STAMPS – Windows on the World'.

The 'Mother Goose' collection consists of two separate products. Each of these is designed as a participative activity book for young children (aged 3 years and upwards) and is based upon the use of popular nursery rhymes. Across the two products the same book metaphor and style of interaction are used reasonably consistently. In many ways these books are similar to the Discis products described in the last section since they are examples of 'talking picture books'. Within each page there are two reactive pictures (see Figure 5.10A); when a user moves the cursor over a particular picture the title of its associated nursery rhyme is spoken out. Selecting a picture by pressing an action button (B1 or B2 in Figure 4.4) causes a jump to be made to the page of the book corresponding to that rhyme (see Figure 5.10B). This contains a sequence of characteristic (cartoon-like) pictures that the user can look at while listening to the words of the nursery rhyme being sung. Subsequently, the user can choose to return to the visual index pages of the book, listen to the same rhyme again or participate in an activity (Figure 5.10C. The activity in 'Mother Goose Hidden Pictures' involves having to find hidden objects within a picture; when these have been successfully located the picture colours itself in and then animates. The activity involved in the other product, 'Mother Goose Rhymes to Colour', is based upon an electronic colouring book. In this book the user is set the task of colouring a picture using an electronic paintbrush. When it is completed the user can animate the picture using the colours he or she has selected.

The 'Stamps' CD is designed as an electronic reference manual containing details of 300 different stamps. The disc embeds over four hours of audio narration, sound effects and colourful reproductions of the stamps. It also contains details of their value, their purpose, denomination, title, country, Scott number and year of issue. The reference book is organized into seven sections:

the hobby of stamp collecting;
your collection;
printing and design;
investing;

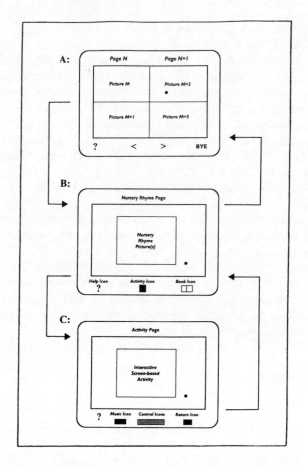

Figure 5.10 *Page hierarchy in CD-I 'Mother Goose' publications*

philatelic follies;
forms of collecting;
specializing.

The 'stamps' contained on the CD can be accessed according to any of three basic views: world, theme or stamp. In the 'world view', a colourful map of the world is displayed on the screen; this can then be used as a table of contents by which stamps can be accessed. For example, moving the cursor to Spain and pressing an action button takes the user to the pages in the album containing the stamp entries for Spain.

The 'theme view' menu takes the form of a picture containing various types of object such as a car, bicycle, aeroplane, various animals and so on. Each object in the picture represents a theme under which stamps have been organized. Selecting the car, for example, would take the user to the section of the album dealing with stamps of 'Cars and Trains'. Similarly, selecting the butterfly in the picture would lead to the pages of the album containing stamps of 'Insects'.

'Stamp view' also provides a pictorial index into the stamp collection. In this view the stamps in the electronic collection are organized into themes that relate specifically to stamps themselves – such as postal history, stamp values, printing methods, early popular stamps, airmail and so on.

There is a substantial volume of hypermedia information on the Stamps CD. Fortunately, all the stamps in the collection and their associated information are interlinked in various ways to form a sophisticated hypermedia knowledge corpus through which the user is encouraged to 'hyper-browse'.

Conclusion

Books have always been and will continue to be a major part of human culture. They provide the means by which information and knowledge are passed from one generation to another. Unfortunately, conventional books that are published on paper suffer from many limitations. In order to overcome these limitations, attempts must be made to find new, more versatile media which will support their publication. A number of candidate media have been described in this chapter – magnetic disc, optical disc and various sorts of electronic media. In this chapter we have referred to books that are published on these dynamic, interactive media as 'electronic books'.

Within this chapter we have considered the basic nature of electronic books and the types of delivery platform needed to access them. The basic techniques involved in designing and producing electronic books have also been considered. A taxonomy of electronic books containing ten different types of book was introduced. Hypermedia electronic books were identified as being of particular importance and their special properties have therefore been described and discussed. A description has been given of a variety of different examples of hypermedia electronic books. These have been published on a range of different media for delivery using a variety of different workstations such as a Macintosh PC, an IBM PC, a multimedia PC, a Sony Data Discman and CD-I equipment.

There is substantial versatility in the range of products that is now available commercially and, undoubtedly, this range of products will expand. Even so, it is highly unlikely that electronic books will ever fully replace their paper-based counterparts. Hopefully, they will co-exist and augment each other's roles as vehicles to support knowledge transfer processes between different groups of people, different societies and different generations.

6 Future Directions

Introduction

For many reasons there is a growing interest in hypertext and hypermedia within a wide range of application areas – particularly education. As we shall discuss later in this chapter, one of the primary reasons for this is the fact that it provides a powerful mechanism through which to implement the currently popular 'constructivist' theory of learning (Cunningham *et al.*, 1993; Merrill, 1991), that is, the view that individual students and groups of learners should be actively involved in constructing knowledge rather than being mere consumers of other people's.

The notion of knowledge construction and sharing is easily accommodated within a hypermedia environment, as is the need to support many different views of knowledge about a given topic or subject (Barker and Proud, 1987). Of course, facile sharing of knowledge, support for different views and active construction necessitate that adequate support technology is put into place. Until now, the technology to support constructivist approaches has been very limited and often inadequate; however, this situation is rapidly changing. It is therefore the intent of this chapter to explore the nature of the changes that are taking place and how these will impact upon the greater realization and utilization of hypermedia techniques, particularly within an educational and training setting.

We commence our exploration of future possibilities by looking at the problems involved in transferring materials from one type of system to another and the ways in which hypermedia resources might become more portable. This, quite naturally, then raises the topic of 'distributed hypermedia', that is, the mechanisms by which users of a global hypermedia knowledge corpus can interlink and access non-linear resources in ways that are independent of the physical locations at which these resources are stored. A natural progression from distributed hypermedia is the use of very sophisticated telecommunications facilities and simulation tools for the realization of 'telepresence' and 'virtual reality' environments, respectively. The relationship of these topics to hypermedia is briefly explored in this chapter.

Another important area that is likely to gain significant prominence in the future is the 'joining together' of artificial intelligence (AI) techniques with hypertext and hypermedia systems (Rada, 1991). The combination of AI methods (such as the use of expert systems and neural networks) must therefore be discussed. Related to this is the use of hypermedia within advanced training products such as electronic performance support systems; this usage is explored in this chapter.

Evaluation is another important (and often very difficult) process that frequently has to be undertaken in order to assess the merits and usefulness of a hypertext/hypermedia facility. Some key points on evaluation are presented at the end of the chapter along with a description of some possible future directions of development for hypermedia systems.

Transferability and portability

The creation of sophisticated hypermedia knowledge corpora depends critically upon the availability of suitable technologies that will support the storage of substantial volumes of dynamic multimedia information (text, pictures and sound); the embedding and accessing of dynamic links within this information; and the easy sharing of the interlinked systems that are ultimately created. Current technology supports each of these requirements to varying extents. However, the problems of sharing hypermedia knowledge across different hardware and software platforms is still a 'sticky' issue. The underlying nature of the problems involved is illustrated schematically in Figure 6.1.

There are three basic issues that must be considered: first,

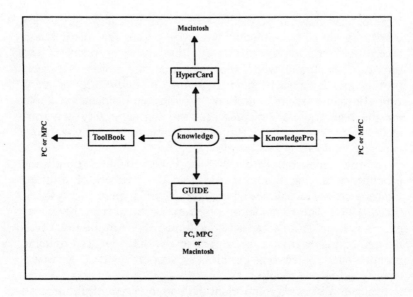

Figure 6.1 *Transferring hypermedia resources between platforms*

choosing a knowledge representation tool within which to encode the knowledge that is to be committed to the selected storage media; second, selecting a hardware platform to enable the creation and delivery of the hypermedia representations of that knowledge; third, identifying a geographic location at which the necessary platform(s) will be located. All of these issues are intimately associated with each other.

The selection of a knowledge representation tool and development/delivery platform are closely-bound decisions in that, very often, a choice made about one determines the other. For example, a decision to use HyperCard to create hypermedia resources implies that a Macintosh computer will be used to create and deliver the resources. Similarly, the selection of an IBM PC (or compatible) or MPC platform implies (in Figure 6.1) that ToolBook, KnowledgePro or GUIDE will be used to develop the knowledge corpus. Having made decisions about authoring tool and hardware platform, a decision then has to be made about the location at which the hypermedia materials will be developed and/or delivered – an office computer (which office, which computer?), a home computer and so on.

Unfortunately, hypermedia resources are still far from transferable between different computer systems. Materials developed for use in one environment cannot easily be used in another. For example, it would not be feasible to author hypermedia resources using HyperCard on an Amiga PC for ultimate delivery on an Apple Macintosh Classic microcomputer. Similarly, a complex hypermedia knowledge corpus that has been created using a powerful SUN Sparcstation could not be taken home from the office and accessed using a Macintosh, an IBM PC, a Sony Data Discman or a CD-I player. These are the sorts of problems of transferability that designers and producers of hypermedia materials currently face and must solve.

The situation is not really as difficult as this implies. There are ways and means of overcoming most of the problems that have been mentioned. For example, one important way of helping to ensure that hypermedia resources are as transferable as possible is to define them in a system-independent way using a technique known as 'meta-level authoring'. The creation of hypermedia using this approach is a two-step process. The first step involves using a special system-independent mark up language (like SGML) in order to specify, in a machine-independent way, how units of information are structured, how they relate to each other and the ways in which they are interlinked. The second step then involves using a series of software conversion tools to process the marked up hypermedia resources and 'port' them to various machine-dependent platforms for delivery to users.

Another way of overcoming the transferability problem is through the sharing of a central resource to which all users can gain access. In this approach the hypermedia corpus is created on a centrally available computer system that can be accessed by users, either via a local area network or by means of a wide area network, using their own microcomputers as interactive terminal devices. In many ways, this approach employs mechanisms which are similar to those used in distributed hypermedia systems of the type that are to be described in the following section.

One other very important issue that has to be considered in relation to transferability is the problem of portability – the ability to physically move a hypermedia corpus from one geographical location to another, thereby making it totally independent of any particular development or delivery site. This requirement is increasingly being fulfilled as a result of the availability of powerful, relatively low-cost, portable computer systems similar to that illustrated in Figure 6.2, which shows a typical notebook computer that contains within it a large capacity, exchangeable hard disc unit. It contains a PCMCIA 'credit card' memory unit which is also exchangeable and can, when necessary, be swapped for a modem card. A computer such as this can easily be connected to a portable CD drive, thereby providing access to CD-ROM discs. Computer facilities of this sort now make it possible for hypermedia knowledge corpora to be made totally portable. Also, through the use of its built-in modem card, a notebook computer of this sort can be attached to a telephone network and can then be used to access remote hypermedia resources virtually anywhere in the world.

In the work that we have recently been doing with portable interactive learning environments (Barker, 1993c) we have been exploring the use of notebook computers (similar to that shown in Figure 6.2) and PCMCIA memory cards as a means of making a number of different hypermedia knowledge corpora portable. We have, for example, installed 'Hypertext Hands-On!' (Shneiderman and Kearsley, 1989) onto a 2Mb hard SRAM (Static Random Access Memory) credit card memory, which means that the whole corpus (and several others) can be carried about in a jacket pocket or in a handbag!

Figure 6.2 *Notebook computer fitted with a PCMCIA memory card*

Distributed hypermedia

As a direct consequence of improved telecommunications and advances in computer networking it is becoming easier and easier to connect different, physically distinct, computer systems together in order to form more sophisticated 'distributed computing facilities'. Users of such systems then have access to a single integrated system whose properties and performance are, in principle, totally independent of the geographical location in which different components reside. Logically, such systems are built up from two basic types of entity: 'servers', that provide a facility or resource for the network system as a whole; and 'clients', that require access to a network facility or consume a network resource. Distributed computing networks that have been designed to function in this way are often called 'client-server' systems.

In the past (and to a large extent even today) most hypertext and hypermedia facilities have been designed as, and are operated as, single user, centralized systems. That is, they reside on a single computer and can be accessed by only one user at a time. However, as was suggested in the previous section, there is an increasing demand to provide various types of distributed hypertext and hypermedia system that will support many users simultaneously. A number of examples of distributed hypermedia system currently exist. Broadly, these fall into two basic categories: single server and multiple server systems (Noll and Scacchi, 1991).

Most of the simplest types of distributed hypertext and hypermedia system employ a single server to store links and nodes for the overall system. Client programs running on workstations connected to the server by a local area network can then access this server to manipulate various portions of the central knowledge corpus. This arrangement is illustrated schematically in Figure 6.3A. Examples of early systems that used this approach include: the Neptune system which was produced by Tektronix (Delisle and Schwartz, 1986); Intermedia (Haan et al., 1992; Yankelovich et al., 1988); DIF – Document Integration Facility (Garg and Scacchi, 1990); and KMS, the Knowledge Management System (Akscyn et al., 1988). In the Neptune system, nodes and links are stored in a single database whereas in the other examples listed the links are stored in a database and the nodes are stored in conventional files.

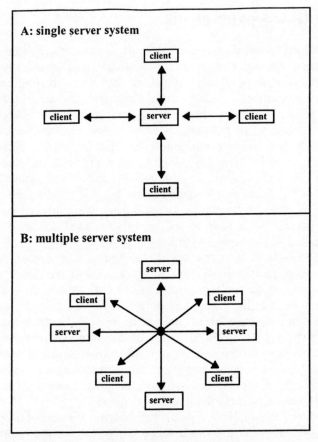

Figure 6.3 *Types of distributed hypermedia system*

In the multiple server approach (which is illustrated schematically in Figure 6.3B), nodes are allowed to reside on several different server machines with links being made between these nodes. Examples of this approach include the Link Service provided by Sun Microsystems (Pearl, 1989), the Virtual Notebook System (Shipman *et al.*, 1989); Distributed DIF; and PlaneText (Conklin, 1987). In most of these systems the links and node locations are stored in a database; however, PlaneText stores both links and nodes in conventional Unix files.

The Neptune system

The Neptune system is an interesting example of a single server distributed hypertext system since it was particularly designed to have an open, layered architecture. It consisted of two basic parts: a front-end (a user-interface written in Smalltalk); and a back-end consisting of a transaction-based server called the 'Hypertext Abstract Machine' (HAM). The HAM was a generic hypertext module which provided operations for creating, modifying and accessing nodes and links. The interface layer provided a range of different browsers, two of the most important of which were the graph browser (which provided a pictorial overview of a sub-graph of nodes and links); and a node browser (for accessing an individual node in a hyperdocument). Other browsers that were provided included: attribute browsers; version browsers; node differences browsers; and demon browsers (a demon is a special section of computer code that is executed when certain types of HAM event take place).

Virtual Notebooks

The Virtual Notebook System (VNS) is a good example of a multiple server system (Shipman *et al.*, 1989). It is a distributed hypertext system that is intended to provide support for work groups in a biomedical setting. In this context, VNS is an electronic analogue to a scientist's notebook; it functions as a repository for data, hypotheses and notes, patient notes and so on. Each notebook consists of a series of pages which can contain text (research notes, electronic mail) or images (graphs and pictures). In many ways these notebooks are similar to the hypermedia electronic books that were discussed in Chapter 5.

The pages that make up a VNS notebook may contain links that make reference to other pages in the hypertext web that makes up a given book. The links that are embedded in pages appear as small icons. They allow rapid movement from one page to another. A link on a page may point to any other page, thereby enabling a single notebook to share pages with other notebooks. In order to create a new link on a page the user simply positions the link on the 'source' page and then clicks the mouse on the 'destination' page.

Information for the new link is stored immediately in the system database and the new link then appears on the source page. A user may work with many notebooks, some of which may be shared by members of his or her immediate workgroup or by other users of the VNS while some notebooks may be private. Users can exchange pages of their notebooks using electronic mail.

The future

The demand for distributed hypermedia systems similar to those described above is likely to grow substantially in future years, as a direct consequence of two important developments. First, there is the growing availability of telecommunications links that are able to support the high-speed exchange of multimedia information between remote sites within a distributed computer network; in this context, the advent of communications facilities based upon the use of ISDN (Integrated Services Digital Network) marks a major step towards the realization of the necessary requirements. Second, there is the commercial release of software to support a distributed approach to designing, creating and using hypermedia systems; already, software that fulfils many of these requirements is starting to appear — 'Lotus Notes', for example, is a software environment that is designed to support distributed group working through the use of electronic mail, multimedia documents and hypertext facilities (Lotus, 1991). Undoubtedly, as more products and services appear, the creation and use of distributed hypermedia systems will become both easier and more popular.

Telepresence and virtual reality

Computer-based information processing technologies bring with them many exciting opportunities for developing innovative approaches to education and training. For example, modern data acquisition equipment, communication facilities and information presentation techniques can be combined in a variety of different ways to enable people to experience phenomena which would otherwise be inaccessible to them. Telepresence and virtual reality (VR) are two important and rapidly developing areas of endeavour which depend upon these technologies Each of these techniques has considerable potential for educational purposes, particularly within the context of experiential learning. This section therefore discusses telepresence and VR and how these might be used to provide access to a range of non-linearly related training and learning activities.

Telepresence

Because human beings are real physical entities, one of their major limitations is their inability to coexist in two different geographical locations simultaneously. Technology can be used in various ways in order to overcome this limitation. Telepresence is one approach that is often employed. The term itself is a generic one that is used to describe mechanisms which enable the presence of an object or process to be projected from one physical location to another by means of appropriate communication channels. Telepresence can be based upon the use of sonic, visual, tactile, multimedia or hypermedia techniques.

One of the most popular methods of implementing telepresence is by means of television. For example, a suitably positioned TV camera can be used to record details of events that are taking place at some particular geographical location; these can then be relayed from the point of capture to viewing locations that can be sited at any distance from the source of the original activity. The most obvious applications of this type of one-way telepresence is in surveillance, monitoring and tracking.

If the TV camera is made mobile (so that it can move from one location to another) then such a system could be used to explore remote terrain or enclosures that might normally be inaccessible to human beings. An arrangement of this sort would obviously require appropriate control procedures to be available for controlling the movement of the camera (called tele-operation). This would mean that a system of two-way telepresence would need to be employed. Two-way telepresence is often used as a basis for building a wide range of remote control applications (Tanifuji et al., 1993). In extremely complex systems, involving a large number of multimedia monitoring points (based upon visual and acoustic sensing), there is a significant need for the design of appropriate hypermedia control interfaces. These are needed to facilitate navigation through the vast quantities of real-time data that are generated and the sophisticated array of control options that is likely to be available within such systems.

Virtual reality

Telepresence techniques enable people to experience multiple realities simultaneously. Some of these realities may be 'artificial' in the sense that they might be generated or transformed by a computer system or some other appropriate agent. A synthetic realism that is generated by a computer system is often referred to as a 'virtual reality'.

One very important limitation of simple telepresence systems (from the point of view of experiential realism) is the fact that the realities that are relayed to a participant often coexist alongside the actual reality in which a participant exists. This therefore acts as a 'frame of reference' which can strongly influence both the physical and the cognitive processes that are involved in using systems of this sort. Therefore, in most VR systems an attempt is made to 'block out' unwanted aspects of the non-synthetic environment in order to enhance the quality of those which are generated artificially. By doing this, it then becomes possible for a user to become totally 'immersed' in an artificial environment that is generated and controlled by a sophisticated computer system (Barker, 1993e; Helsel and Roth, 1991; Krueger, 1991).

An important property of a VR system is the fact that through the immersion processes mentioned above, a human element in the system becomes an active participant within a sophisticated interactive real-time simulation. This simulation depends heavily upon the use of 3-dimensional computer graphics and animation (for generating the objects and scenes within the VR system) and special types of 3-dimensional interaction peripherals to enable human activity to be tracked and the virtuality to be experienced in the correct way. Typical examples of such interaction peripherals include data gloves, body suites and head-mounted displays (Helsel and Roth, 1991).

Using VR and telepresence techniques it is possible to provide a wide range of learning experiences that would not otherwise be feasible. It is also possible to use VR techniques as a substitute for 'real experiences' in situations where it might be too costly or too dangerous to risk exposing students to non-synthetic realities. As an example of what can be done, consider the situation illustrated schematically in Figure 6.4.

This shows a collection of artificial environments (or 'cyberspaces') that have been linked together to produce a non-linear 'hyperspace' system. The system is designed to support the teaching of practical experimental physics. The VR system therefore

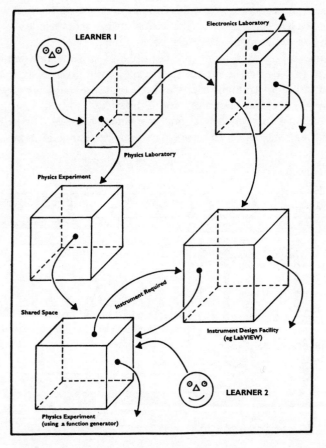

Figure 6.4 *Shared cyberspaces within a virtual reality system*

provides a simulated laboratory environment that one or more students can enter, perhaps to work together in a collaborative way on a particular experiment. As students 'walk' around the laboratory they can choose the particular experiments that they wish to undertake. All the laboratory services and equipment are simulated using sophisticated interactive computer programs. For example, some of the experiments might require students to build specific pieces of electronic equipment that can be used to create different types of signal for input into particular pieces of apparatus. To do this, a virtual instrument laboratory or workbench would probably be used. Such a facility would contain a kit of parts that would enable students to construct the virtual instruments needed for use within the experiments they are conducting.

Figure 6.5 shows a simple example of a simulated function generator. It depicts a typical front-panel and output display trace from a virtual instrument that was built using the LabVIEW system – LabVIEW is an acronym for Laboratory Virtual Instrument Engineering Workbench (National Instruments, 1992). The settings of the four controls on the front-panel can be changed interactively

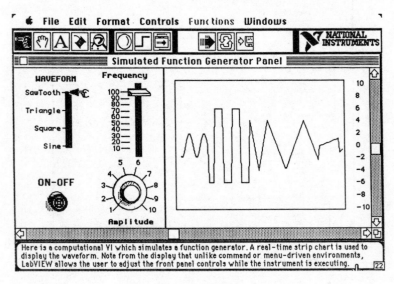

Figure 6.5 *The LabVIEW system*

using mouse-based 'point and click' and 'point and drag' operations. As the user changes the positions of these controls, the output shown in the display area changes dynamically to reflect the new settings.

Future possibilities

For a variety of practical, economic and pedagogic reasons there is likely to be increased use of VR systems for educational purposes in the future. Obviously, hypermedia techniques (particularly those related to navigation) will play both a natural and inherent role within such systems.

Introducing intelligence

There is a variety of ways in which artificial intelligence (AI) techniques and hypermedia methods can be combined. One possibility is to use AI methods to improve the performance and functionality of hypertext systems. Another is to use hypertext and hypermedia methods to improve the quality of AI products such as expert systems. Each of these possibilities is briefly discussed in this section.

Expert systems have become an extremely popular way of applying AI methods to problem solving using what are known as 'knowledge-based methods' (Hart, 1986). Most of the commonly available expert systems model domain knowledge in terms of collections of 'if-then-else' rules. Essentially, these constitute a decision tree which, given the necessary input parameters, reduces a given problem space to more manageable proportions and then provides relevant advice about the problem being solved.

Intelligent hypermedia

In his book, Rada (1991) discusses the possibility of combining an expert system with a hypertext system in order to produce a new type of product which he refers to as an 'expertext' system. Such systems embed expert system features which enable users to find more easily information relevant to their particular needs.

Typical ways in which an expert system might help to improve the quality and usability of a hypertext/hypermedia system are through the use of 'dynamic profiles' in order to model a particular aspect of a user's interests; and by means of various types of support tool for creating and handling the knowledge embedded in a hypermedia system.

The way in which a user profile might be used is illustrated schematically in Figure 6.6. In this illustration, different aspects of a particular user's interests are represented by a series of profiles. These are formed by bringing together a collection of rules that describe his or her specific information interests. The rules from which the profiles are constructed each form an expert system definition which can be used to guide its owner towards particular sections of a hypermedia knowledge corpus that might be most useful in the context of the problem currently being addressed. An example of the way in which user-modelling (or profiling) can be

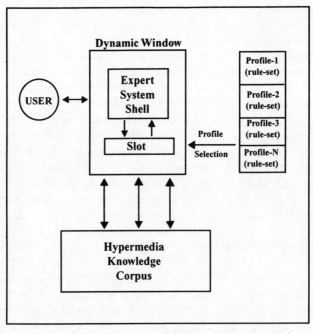

Figure 6.6 *Use of an expert system for hypermedia profiling*

used was illustrated in Figure 4.3. This showed how built-in intelligence could be used to maintain a multi-level knowledge corpus for the different types of staff involved in a commercial organization.

Support tools for use in hypermedia systems fall into two basic categories – those used for design purposes and those used to facilitate access, retrieval and navigation. Hamlin and Stemp (1990) have described a useful collection of AI-based methods to support the design of hypertext and hypermedia systems. They base their design on the use of 'semantic networks' (Hart, 1986). Within a given domain, these are used to identify concepts and the links that connect them into propositions. They then use a set of three 'scaling algorithms' to: a) produce spatial representations of conceptual knowledge; b) help determine the dimensions which underlie these concepts; and c) graphically illustrate how these concepts are linked in a human expert's memory. The three tools used to analyse the relationships between concepts are the multidimensional scaling (MDS) algorithm; cluster analysis; and the Pathfinder algorithm. MDS is used to produce a map of the 'semantic distance' of concepts in memory. Cluster analysis is used to show how concepts are judged as belonging together in groups. The Pathfinder algorithm then takes an individual concept, lists each of the concepts to which it is linked and shows the strength and intensity of these relationships.

Another interesting aspect of 'intelligent support' for hypermedia has been described by Kibby and Mayes (1989). They discuss ways of automatically computing the degrees of relatedness between the member nodes of a hypertext system. They believe that the use of explicit hard coded links in hypertext and hypermedia would ultimately be a limiting factor in the construction of large systems. Consequently, in their StrathTutor system (see Chapter 4) they did not emphasize the use of fixed links, although the system did contain some. Instead, they preferred to use dynamic links that were calculated (from similarity measures) as a user was actually using their system. The success of Kibby and Mayes' StrathTutor system depended upon the use of a computer model for human memory called MINERVA. This involved the use of associative recall based upon the use of classification attributes.

Augmenting AI techniques

Examples of the ways in which hypermedia methods can be used to augment AI techniques have been given by Barker (1989a; 1992f) and Carlson and Ram (1990). In his work, Barker describes the use of both KnowledgePro and Prolog as a means of building expert systems that embed non-linearly organized multimedia material that can be delivered to users during consultation dialogues. He found the use of the KnowledgePro system particularly useful for creating expert systems involving hypertext and reactive graphical images. These images could be of a static nature or based upon the use of full- or partial-screen motion video.

Carlson and Ram also describe various ways in which hypermedia methods and AI techniques can be combined. They discuss how mental models may be used to organize an individual's thoughts while formatting a strategic plan. They describe a hypermedia-AI system called SPRINT (an acronym for 'Strategic Plan and Resource INTegration') which can be used by a manager to make implicit plans more explicit. Users of SPRINT can create concept nodes and links which describe their understanding of the business environment impacting a particular strategic plan. In addition, the user can specify the resources that are required to achieve the plan and the relationship that these resources hold with the strategies. The system design for this product involved two significant features: the use of integrated heuristic rules, and the use of goal oriented communication between the models of individual managers. The prototype system for SPRINT was written using an object-orientated language (Smalltalk/V) and was designed to run on an IBM PC/AT.

Future possibilities

A wide range of new AI methods is becoming available for use in hypermedia systems. Two of the most promising techniques that have recently emerged from research into AI are 'fuzzy logic' and 'neural network' systems. Fuzzy logic is useful for representing imprecise concepts. There are many situations in which we have an imprecise view or understanding of the nature of the information that we wish to extract from a hypermedia system. Such situations are ideally suited for modelling using a fuzzy logic approach. Neural network systems represent a major step forward with respect to automatic problem solving since they can 'learn' how to solve particular types of problem (Hedberg, 1993). The way in which we are using neural networks within hypermedia systems is briefly discussed in the following section.

Performance support systems

In several places within this book reference has been made to performance support systems (see, for example, Chapters 1 and 4). We return to a discussion of this topic here because of the potential future role of electronic performance support technology in online training and the place that hypermedia is likely to have within EPSS facilities.

The history of EPSS lies rooted in the development of electronic job aids and human performance support tools (Gery, 1991; Raybould, 1990; Rossett, 1991). The industrial and commercial importance of such systems lies in the fact that they

> will provide all employees with access to a training workstation at or near their desk. If their job involves working on a computer such as customer service or airline reservations, the performance support will be integrated into the actual automated system on which they work. (Heathman and Kleiner, 1991).

A performance support system is essentially a 'job aid' that enables its users to improve the efficiency and effectiveness with which they are able to complete particular job tasks within some application domain. A simple example of a performance support system is a 'pocket calculator'; this device enables its user to perform complex calculations which could not otherwise easily be undertaken. Word processing systems and desktop publishing packages are further examples of performance support systems since they significantly improve the efficiency with which their users can create documentation. E-mail and computer-supported cooperative work (CSCW) techniques are also important job performance aids since they enable geographically distributed organizations to undertake rapid inter-site and inter-personal communication, to share important intellectual and managerial resources and to participate in collaborative problem solving at a distance.

Our approach to the provision of EPSS facilities is based upon the use of a generic architecture which is illustrated schematically in Figure 6.7. Essentially, there are four basic levels to consider. At the topmost level there are two 'compulsory' functional units: the human-computer interface and the support database. Within level 2 the system designer can choose from a range of different optional generic support tools for the EPSS. At this level, the particular types of system component that are incorporated into any particular implementation will depend upon the nature of the application and the function that the EPSS is to perform within the organization. The various components at level 3 of the architecture are application oriented tools. These may already exist within the particular application domain or they may need to be specifically

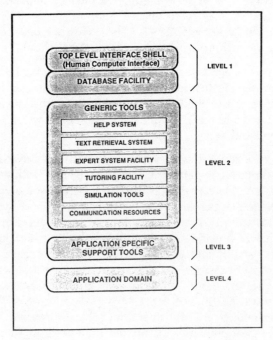

Figure 6.7 *Generic architecture for an EPSS*

built for the application. At the lowest level of the architecture we find the target application system for which the EPSS is being built.

One important aspect of EPSS design and implementation that we have been exploring is the provision of organizational documentation in electronic form. This requirement is necessary for a number of practical reasons – primarily, the large volumes of information that are involved and the ease with which electronic documentation can be accessed, updated and shared. As part of our EPSS research we have therefore been exploring the problems involved in converting conventional paper-based documentation into both linearly and non-linearly organized electronic forms.

As an alternative publication medium we have been using CD-ROM to produce a series of electronic books for use within a distributed performance support system based upon the use of the ISDN (Integrated Services Digital Network). The topology of the system we have been considering is similar to that depicted schematically in Figure 6.8. The implementation depends upon the creation of three basic types of electronic book publication: common shared books, private local books and external public books. These contain textual information, multimedia information and hypermedia material. The electronic publications embed the information necessary to facilitate many different aspects of organizational activity, ranging from technical support through to management decision making. A range of information storage and retrieval techniques have been employed in order to provide access to the stored information that is held on the CD-ROM discs.

Our recent work with distributed performance support systems has been orientated towards the design of mobile 'intelligent agents' to facilitate knowledge sharing (Barker, Richards and Banerji, 1993). Within our system these intelligent agents are used to keep track of an organization's expertise within different problem solving domains. In time-critical situations these agents can be used to locate sources of relevant expertise and to facilitate the transfer of this expertise (in electronic form) to the required point of need.

The intelligent agents are constructed from expert systems and neural networks. The expert systems embed 'common sense' rules of inferencing while the neural networks are used to represent windows onto 'deep' compiled knowledge that provide different perspectives on the common, shared knowledge resources

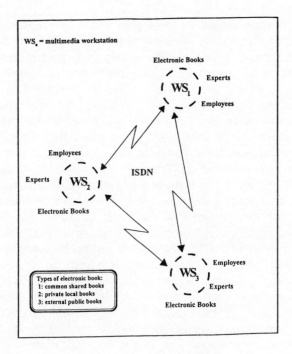

Figure 6.8 *A distributed EPSS*

contained within an organization. The attractive feature of using neural networks as a navigation aid within linear and non-linear knowledge corpora is the fact that they can learn about and adapt dynamically to a user's particular information requirements.

Future possibilities

Many industrial and commercial organizations are starting to employ EPSS facilities because of the potential benefits that they can offer with respect to improvements in productivity and competitiveness. Increasingly, there is a tendency to use hypermedia techniques within these systems because of the flexible ways in which hypermedia methods enable information to be accessed (Dean *et al.*, 1993). However, an important problem that will need to be solved in the future will be the conversion of an organization's conventional documentation into hypertext and hypermedia format (Rada, 1992). We shall return to a discussion of this topic in the final section.

Evaluation

Hypermedia materials take a wide variety of forms and can be used for a range of different purposes. The evaluation of a given hypermedia product is therefore important for a number of different reasons. For example, typical questions that might be asked of it could include:

Is it valid for its purpose?
Does it meet educational training aims?
Does it offer value for money?
Is it usable?
Is it suitable for its intended audience?
What is its expected lifetime?

Also, if the product is aimed at an educational market, it is important to know if it is pedagogically sound, relevant to the target curriculum, written at an appropriate level and so on.

Types of evaluation

Hypermedia products can be subjected to a wide range of different types of evaluation. Brief descriptions of some of the most popular of these have been presented by Knussen et al., (1991). The six evaluation models that they describe are: the classical experimental model; the research and development model; the illuminative model; the briefing decision-maker's model; the teacher as researcher model; and the case study model. Bearing in mind the different purposes and scopes of these models, Knussen et al. suggest that 'there is no single path for the potential evaluator to follow'. They further suggest that:

At the outset, the evaluator must be clear about the aims and objectives of the evaluation, the resources that are available, the audience of reports, and the decisions that will result from the reports. All evaluations are limited in some way, and it is up to evaluators to take account of these limitations.

Most of the conventional approaches to product evaluation fall into two broad categories: formative and summative.

Formative evaluation is orientated towards the development phase of product creation; it is concerned with the progress being made in achieving the goals of a product during its implementation. Its aim is primarily to identify any changes that are needed during its development in order to keep the product on course. The way in which formative evaluation can be used to good effect is illustrated in the design and development work reported in the SuperBook project (Landauer *et al.*, 1993). Hutchings, Hall and Colbourn (1992) have also described an extensive quantitative study of student's interaction with an educational hypermedia system in which formative methods were used to improve the quality of the final product.

In contrast to the above approach, summative evaluation is primarily concerned with the quality and effectiveness of a product in terms of its stated aims and objectives. Typically, summative evaluation would be used to assess the overall quality of a product; its suitability for particular types of tasks and categories of user; and, how well it compares with other products that may already be in use. A typical example of a summative evaluation can be seen in the work of Smeaton (1991). He studied the usage of a hypertext product by undergraduate students alongside conventional books and lectures. Students were surveyed on when and how they used the hypertext, for what specific purposes and what types of searching they preferred.

Evaluation tools

A range of different tools is available for conducting evaluations. These vary in sophistication from informal review techniques through to controlled experiments involving pre-test and post-test activities. Knussen *et al.* (1991) have presented and discussed a useful summary of some of the more important categories of evaluation tool. The ones they consider include:
* systematic observation;

- use of self-report techniques;
- interview methods;
- automated methods;
- use of psychometric tests;
- use of design guidelines and checklists; and
- purpose designed evaluation experiments.

Conducting any realistic large-scale evaluation is a very difficult and time-consuming process that is subject to a wide range of environmental factors. Automated methods are very useful since they can be used to collect a wide range of data in an unobtrusive way using a monitoring mechanism that is actually built into the product or runs alongside it. Knussen *et al.* (1991), for example, describe the use of a system called 'AutoMonitor' which is a software tool to facilitate automated data collection relating to HyperCard systems. It creates a time-stamped record of each of the cards viewed during a particular user's use of the system. Such records can be analysed statistically and interpreted in conjunction with any other observations (such as video tape records or informal observations) taken during the evaluation.

Future directions

Despite the fact that hypermedia systems have been available for some considerable time there seem to be few really well-established, easy-to-use procedures for their evaluation. Most of this type of work is time-consuming, costly and prone to errors. For this reason, evaluation often does not get done or gets done in a very superficial way. The effective evaluation of hypermedia systems – see, for example, Hutchings, Hall and Colbourn (1992) – is necessary to prove that they work and to establish useful guidelines for their future production. A laudable goal for the future of hypermedia would be the identification of some useful evaluation goals and the establishment of a set of procedures by which these might be realized.

What next?

In this final section of 'Exploring Hypermedia' an attempt is made to summarize some of the more important aspects of hypermedia which might influence its future development and use.

Learning to write

Many of the tasks involved in designing and writing hypermedia documents are quite complex, both conceptually and practically. This complexity arises because of the large number of design options that are available and the wide range of factors that can influence the way in which a hypermedia message can unfold. The process of non-linear writing is further complicated by the fact that most authors are so familiar with designing and writing conventional texts that turning their skills to non-linear documents is not an easy process. Undoubtedly, in the future we will need sets of well-documented, easy-to-follow rules and guidelines to help us create non-linear documents in an effective and efficient way.

New books for old

We have available in our libraries a significant number of conventional books and vast quantities of audio-visual material. For a variety of reasons (such as shared simultaneous access, ease of searching, security of documents and so on), it would be convenient if this material could be made available in electronic form. Such a transition could be used to preserve the structure of the materials involved, and their basic inter-relationships, through the use of the book metaphors that have been described earlier in this book. Once the information is in electronic form, as well as preserving the original formats, new hyper-linked productions could also be produced. Some initial explorations into converting a conventional textbook into hypertext format have been made by Rada (1992) and Barker *et al.* (1993). However these investigations have only scratched the surface; there is considerable scope for further work in this very important area.

End-user interface design

End-user interaction with a hypermedia product takes place through the medium of the product's human-computer interface subsystem (Barker, 1989b). The design of 'quality' interfaces to hypermedia materials is therefore of paramount importance if they are to be used in efficient and effective ways. Wright (1989) has considered some of the interface alternatives for use in hypertext systems. In discussing the options available she comments:

> ... decisions are both more numerous and more complex than the decision-making required when creating conventional printed texts. Some hypertext systems retain a close similarity to linear printed text, although coupling the text with other functionality. . . . Other hypertext generators allow authors to provide the reader with totally novel information structures, structures in which they are able to do things which have no counterpart in printed media. Here the design of the interface becomes more demanding, and there will be no simple guidelines to assist authors in the choices they make.

The production of a set of sound human-computer interface design guidelines for use in hypermedia systems will be an important step towards the realization of easier access to and production of hypermedia resources.

New approaches to knowledge sharing

Some of the advantages of making information and knowledge available in electronic form have already been listed earlier in this section. Another important advantage of providing facilities of this sort is the fact that they would support many new approaches to learning (see below) and the sharing of knowledge. Consider, for example, a library in 'electronic form' (Catenazi, Landoni and Gibb, 1993). Such a library becomes one in which virtually all its books and research journals could be made 'instantly' available to anyone who wants to see them. These items become accessible both by local readers and those who are located remotely. By hyper-linking references and citations in one electronic text to their corresponding source documents it becomes easier to access these directly, if and when the need arises. Key ideas and concepts in one document could also be linked, by users, to corresponding ideas and concepts located in other documents, thereby making it easier to compare and contrast different interpretations of data and facts. A similar argument applies to the documents contained within virtually all organizations; having these in electronic form and hyper-linked improves access and the ease with which they, or sections of them, can be shared. As systems of this type start to become more widely available, so we move more closely to the kinds of hypertext and hypermedia facilities envisaged by early pioneers of this technique such as Bush, Engelbart and Nelson (see Chapter 1).

New ways to study

Hypermedia, through the use of interactive technologies, enables the realization of many new approaches to learning. Currently, one of the most popular is 'constructivism' – the view that students should be actively involved in knowledge construction processes. Cunningham *et al.* (1993) define this approach in the following way:

> the goal of constructivist instruction is to aid the student in gaining the capability to ask relevant questions, to generate authentic contexts for the use of knowledge to guide the interpretation of the information, to test his or her views against alternative views, and to become aware of the knowledge construction process.

Currently available computer-based information technologies provide a rich resource for the realization of the above requirements. In the context of the constructivist approach to learning, Duffy and Knuth (1990) have described the potential of hypertext and hypermedia in the following way: hypermedia technology seems ideally suited to supporting constructivist learning environments. Duffy and Knuth's strong support for hypermedia stems from the facilities it offers for the use of link processes, authoring and collaboration.

For centuries, conventional books have been the mainstay of education. The constructivist theory does not preclude their use but forces us to bear in mind their limitations: being geared to knowledge telling rather than knowledge construction. In their deliberations on *The Textbook of the Future*, Cunningham, *et al.* (1993) suggest:

the combination of technology and constructivism, however, offers possibilities undreamed of until recently. We believe that the most important idea presented here is the notion that the textbook of the future will be a construction of the learner, drawing upon the database and authoring, linking and customising tools provided.

Final remarks

This book was written as an introductory text to guide readers' explorations of this new and exciting area of educational technology. Within the space available it has not been possible to cover topics in great depth or to be in any way comprehensive in approach. However, it is my belief that this book will provide a sufficiently robust skeleton to which readers can themselves add flesh and substance as they further explore the potential and utility of hypermedia within their own application areas.

References

Akscyn, RM, McCracken, DL and Yoder, EA (1988) 'KMS: a distributed hypermedia system for managing knowledge in large organisations', *Communications of the ACM*, **31**,7, 820–35.

Ambron, S and Hooper, K (1990) (eds) *Learning with Interactive Multimedia – Developing and Using Multimedia Tools in Education*, Redmond, WA: Microsoft Press.

Asymetrix (1989a) *Using ToolBook – A Guide to Building and Working with Books*, Bellevue, WA: Asymetrix Corporation.

Asymetrix (1989b) *Using OpenScript – An Introduction and Reference to the OpenScript Language*, Bellevue, WA: Asymetrix Corporation.

Baird, P (1990) 'Hypertext – towards the single intellectual market', in Nielson, J (ed.) *Designing User Interfaces for International Use*, volume 14 in Advances in Human Factors/Ergonomics, Amsterdam: Elsevier.

Banerji, AK (1993) 'Designing Electronic Performance Support Systems', draft PhD thesis, University of Teesside, Cleveland.

Barker, PG (1987) *Author Languages for CAL*, Basingstoke: Macmillan Education.

Barker, PG (1989a) 'KnowledgePro: a review and assessment', *Engineering Applications of Artificial Intelligence*, **2**,4, 325–38.

Barker, PG (1989b) *Basic Principles of Human-Computer Interface Design*, London: Century-Hutchinson.

Barker, PG (1989c) *Multimedia Computer-Assisted Learning*, London: Kogan Page.

Barker, PG (1990) 'Electronic books', *Learning Resources Journal*, **6**,3, 62–8.

Barker, PG (1991a) 'Interactive electronic books', *Interactive Multimedia*, **2**,1, 11–28.

Barker, PG (1991b) 'Electronic Books', special edition of *Educational and Training Technology International*, **28**,4, 269–368.

Barker, PG (1992a) 'An object oriented approach to hypermedia authoring', in Giardina, M (ed.) *Interactive Multimedia Learning Environments*, NATO ASI Series F: Computer and Systems Sciences, volume 93, Berlin: Springer-Verlag.

Barker, PG (1992b) 'Design guidelines for electronic book production', in Edwards, ADN and Holland, S (eds) *Multimedia Interface Design in Education*, NATO ASI Series F: Computer and Systems Sciences, volume 76, Berlin: Springer-Verlag.

Barker, PG (1992c) 'Electronic books and libraries of the future', *The Electronic Library*, **10**,3, 139–49.

Barker, PG (1992d) 'Hypermedia electronic books', in *Proceedings of the Seventh Canadian Symposium on Instructional Technology*, Montreal: Canadian Association of Coarseware Producers.

Barker, PG (1992e) 'Electronic books and their potential for international distance learning', invited paper presented at the East-West Conference on 'Emerging Computer Technologies in Education', Moscow, 6–9 April 1992.

Barker, PG (1992f) 'Using pictures in expert systems', *Engineering Applications of Artificial Intelligence*, **5**,4, 329–44.

Barker, PG (1993a) *Hypermedia for Teaching, Project Overview*, Interactive Systems Research Group, School of Computing and Mathematics, University of Teesside, Cleveland.

Barker, PG (1993b) 'Pictorial communication', in *Proceedings of the International Conference on Non-Visual Human Computer Interaction – Prospects for the Visually Handicapped*, Colloque INSERM, volume 228, Paris: John Libby Eurotext.

Barker, PG (1993c) 'Portable interactive learning environments', in Estes, N and Thomas, M (eds) *Volume 1 of Proceedings of the 10th International Conference on Technology and Education – Rethinking the Roles of Technology in Education*, Austin, Texas: the University of Texas.

Barker, PG (1993d) 'The design of electronic book emulators', paper to be presented to the 11th International Conference on Technology and Education, Imperial College, London.

Barker, PG (1993e) 'Virtual reality: theoretical basis, practical applications', *Journal of the Association for Learning Technology*, **1**,1, 15–25.

Barker, PG and Banerji, AK (1993a) 'Designing electronic

performance support systems', in Estes, N and Thomas, M (eds) *Volume 1 of Proceedings of the 10th International Conference on Technology and Education — Rethinking the Roles of Technology in Education*, Boston, MA. 21–4 March 1993.

Barker, PG and Banerji, AK (1993b) 'Multimedia environments for EPSS development', in Balagurusamy, E and Sushila, B (eds) *Proceedings of the Indian Computing Congress (ICC '92) — Innovative Applications in Computing*, New Delhi: Tata McGraw-Hill Publishing Company.

Barker, PG and Giller, S (1991) 'An electronic book for early learners', *Educational and Training Technology International*, **28**,4, 140–60.

Barker, PG and Giller, S (1992a) *Design Guidelines for Electronic Book Production — Overview Report*, Interactive Systems Research Group, School of Computing and Mathematics, University of Teesside, Cleveland.

Barker, PG and Giller, S (1992b) *Design Guidelines for Electronic Book Production, Final Project Report*, submitted to the Learning Technology Unit, Training, Enterprise and Education Directorate, Department of Employment, Moorfoot, Sheffield.

Barker, PG and Giller, S (1992c) 'Electronic books', in Saunders, D and Race, P (eds) *Aspects of Educational Technology, Volume XXV: Developing and Measuring Competence*, London: Kogan Page.

Barker, PG and Giller, S (1992d) 'Electronic books for distance learning', in Estes, N and Thomas, M (eds) *Volume 2 of the Proceedings of the Ninth International Conference on Technology and Education*, Austin, Texas: University of Texas.

Barker, PG and Manji, KA (1988) 'New books for old', *Programmed Learning and Educational Technology*, **25**,4, 310–13.

Barker, PG and Manji, KA (1990) 'Designing electronic books', *Journal of Artificial Intelligence in Education*, **1**,2, 31–42.

Barker, PG and Proud, A (1987) 'A practical introduction to authoring for computer assisted instruction. Part 10: knowledge-based CAL', *British Journal of Educational Technology*, **18**,2, 140–60.

Barker, PG, Richards, S and Banerji, AK (1993) 'Intelligent approaches to performance support', in Balagurusamy, E and Sushila, B (eds) *Proceedings of the Indian Computing Conference (ICC '93)*, New Delhi: Tata McGraw-Hill.

Barker, PG, Giller, S, Lamont, C, Richards, S and Dudek, E (1993) 'Thesis publication on CD-ROM', in Estes, N and Thomas, M (eds) *Volume 1 of Proceedings of the 10th International Conference on Technology and Education – Rethinking the Roles of Technology in Education*, Austin, Texas: University of Texas.

Begoray, JA (1990), 'An introduction to hypermedia issues, systems and application areas', *International Journal of Man-Machine Studies*, **33**, 121–47.

Beilby, M (1992) 'Asymetrix ToolBook 1.5', *The CTISS File*, **13**, 16–18.

Bell, GG, O'Connor, JJ and Robertson, GF (1990) 'A mathematics tutorial system', *The CTISS File*, **9**, 13–16.

Bergman, RE and Moore, TV (1990) *Managing Interactive Video/Multimedia Projects*, Englewood Cliffs, NJ: Educational Technology Publications.

Bogaerts, WF and Agema, KS (1992) 'Active Library on Corrosion', Amsterdam: Elsevier Science Publishers.

Bolt, R (1980) '"Put That There": voice and gesture at the graphics interface', *Computer Graphics*, **14**,3, 262–70.

Brand, S (1988) *The Media Lab: Inventing the Future at MIT*, Harmondsworth: Penguin Books.

Britannica Software (1990) 'Compton's Multimedia Encyclopedia (DOS Version)', San Francisco, CA: Britannica Software, Inc.

Britannica Software (1991) 'Compton's Multimedia Encyclopedia (Windows Version)', San Francisco, CA: Britannica Software, Inc.

Brown, PJ (1986a) 'Interactive documentation', *Software Practice and Experience*, **16**,3, 291–9.

Brown, PJ (1986b) 'Viewing documents on a screen', in Lambert, S and Ropiequet, S (eds) *CD-ROM: The New Papyrus*, Redmond, WA: Microsoft Press.

Bush, V (1945) 'As we may think', *Atlantic Monthly*, **176**,1, 101–8.

CACM (1988) *Communications of the Association of Computing Machinery*, special edition on hypertext, **31**,7, 816–95.

Carlson, DA and Ram, S (1990) 'HyperIntelligence: the next frontier', *Communications of the ACM*, **33**,3, 311–21.

Carroll, JM, Mack, RL and Kellogg, WA (1988) 'Interface metaphors and user interface design', in Helander, M (ed.) *Handbook of Human-Computer Interaction*, New York: Elsevier Science Publishers.

Catenazi, N, Landoni, M and Gibb, F (1993) 'Design issues in the production of hyper-books and visual books', *Journal of the Association of Learning Technology*, **1**,2.

Conklin, J (1987) 'Hypertext: a survey and introduction', *IEEE Computer*, **20**,9, 17–41.

Coulouris, G and Thimbleby, H (1992) *HyperProgramming – Building Interactive Programs with HyperCard*, Wokingham: Addison-Wesley.

Crichton, M (1991) 'Jurassic Park', Santa Monica, CA: The Voyager Company.

CTISS (1990) *The CTISS File*, special edition on hypertext, **9**, February.

Cunningham, DJ, Duffy, TM and Knuth, RA (1993) 'The textbook of the future', in McKnight, C, Dillon, A and Richardson, J (eds) *Hypertext: a Psychological Perspective*, Ellis Horwood Series in Interactive Information Systems, Chichester: Ellis Horwood.

Dean, C and Whitlock, Q (1992) *A Handbook of Computer-Based Training*, 3rd edn, London: Kogan Page.

Dean, C, Watt, C, Whitlock, Q and Wilkinson, S (1993) 'Hypermedia and Performance Support', in Maurer, H (ed.) *Proceedings of ED-MEDIA '93*, Virginia, USA: Association for the Advancement of Computing in Education.

Deegan, M, Timbrell, N and Warren, L (1992) *Hypermedia in the Humanities*, Universities of Oxford and Hull: Information Training Technology Initiative.

Delisle, NM and Schwartz, MD (1986) 'Neptune – a hypertext system for CAD applications', *SIGMOD Record*, **15**,2, 132–42.

Discis (1992) Discis Knowledge Research Inc, 45 Sheppard Avenue East, Suite 410, Toronto, Ontario, Canada M2N 5W9.

Duffy, TM and Knuth, RA (1990) 'Hypermedia and instruction: where is the match?', in Jonasson, D and Mandl, H (eds) *Designing Hypermedia for Learning*, NATO ASI Series F: Computer and Systems Sciences, volume 67, Berlin: Springer-Verlag.

Engelbart, DC (1963) 'A conceptual framework for the augmentation of man's intellect', in Howerton, PD and Weeks, DC (eds) *Vistas in Information Handling, Volume 1*, Washington, DC: Spartan Books.

Engelbart, DC (1984) 'Authorship provisions in augment, COMPCON '84 Digest', in *Proceedings of COMPCON Conference*, February 27–March 1, 1984.

Engelbart, DC and English, WK (1968) 'A research centre for augmenting human intellect', in *AFIPS Conference Proceedings, Volume 33, Part 1*, Washington, DC: The Thompson Book Company.

Entwistle, N (1981) *Styles of Learning and Teaching*, New York: John Wiley.

Ford, N (1985) 'Learning styles and strategies for postgraduate students', *British Journal of Educational Technology*, **16**,1, 17–26.

Garg, PK and Scacchi, W (1990) 'A hypertext system for software life cycle documents', *IEEE Software*, **7**,3, 90–99.

Gery, GJ (1991) *Electronic Performance Support Systems: How and Why to Remake the Workplace through the Strategic Application of Technology*, Boston, MA: Weingarten Publications.

Gibbons, H (1992) ' "Murder One" – developing interactive simulations for teaching law,' *The CTISS File*, **14**, 24–8.

Giller, S (1992) 'Design Guidelines for Electronic Book Production', MPhil thesis, University of Teesside, Cleveland.

Goodman, D (1987) *The Complete HyperCard*, New York: Bantam Books.

Grolier Inc. (1988) *The New Grolier Encyclopedia – User's Guide*, Sherman Turnpike, Danbury, CT: Grolier Electronic Publishing Inc.

Haan, BJ, Kahn, P, Riley, VA, Coombs, JH and Meyrowitz, NK (1992) 'Iris hypermedia services', *Communications of the ACM*, **35**,1, 36–51.

Halasz, FG (1988) 'Reflections on NoteCards: seven issues for the next generation of hypermedia systems', *Communications of the ACM*, **31**,7, 836–52.

Hall, W (1993) The Microcosm Project, contact address: Department of Electronics and Computer Science, University of Southampton, Highfield, Southampton, Hants S09 5NH.

Hamlin, MDB and Stemp, GM (1990) 'The missing link: the use of scaling algorithms to design hypertext instructional materials', in Estes, N, Heene, J and Leclercq, D (eds) *Volume 1 of Proceedings of the Seventh International Conference on Technology and Education – Pathways to Learning Through Educational Technology*, Austin, Texas: The University of Texas.

Hammond, N and Allinson, L (1987) 'The travel metaphor as design principle and training aid for navigating around complex systems', in Diaper, D and Winder, R (eds) *People and Computers III*, Cambridge: Cambridge University Press.

Harrison, N (1991) *How to Design Effective Computer-Based Training*, Maidenhead: McGraw-Hill.

Hart, A (1986) *Knowledge Acquisition for Expert Systems*, London: Kogan Page.

Heathman, DJ and Kleiner, BH (1991) 'Future directions for computer-aided training', *Industrial and Commercial Training*, **23**,5, 25–31.

Hedberg, S (1993) 'New Knowledge Tools', *BYTE*, **18**,8, 106–11.

Helicon Publishing (1992) 'Hutchinson's Guide to the World, Electronic Book Version 1.0', London: Helicon Publishing.

Helsel, SK and Roth, JP (1991) *Virtual Reality – Theory, Practice and Promise*, Westport, CT: Meckler.

Hewett, TT (1987) 'The Drexel Disc: an electronic guidebook', in Diaper, D and Winder, R (eds) *People and Computers III*, Proceedings of the Third Conference of the British Computer Society Human-Computer Interaction Specialist Group, University of Exeter, 7–11 September, Cambridge: Cambridge University Press.

Horn, RE (1989) *Mapping Hypertext: Analysis, Linkage and Display of Knowledge for the Next Generation of On-Line Text and Graphics*, Lexington, MA: The Lexington Institute.

Horn, RE (1992) 'Opinion: clarifying two controversies about information mapping's method', *Educational and Training Technology International*, **29**,2, 109–17.

Horney, MA and Anderson-Inman, L (1993) 'Reading in hypertext: new skills for a new context', in Estes, N and Thomas, M (eds) *Proceedings of the 10th International Conference on Technology and Education*, vol 1, Austin, Texas: The University of Texas.

Hutchings, GA, Hall, W and Colbourn, CJ (1992) *A Quantitative Study of Students' Interactions with a Hypermedia System, Technical Report CSTR 92-04*, Southampton: Department of Electronics and Computer Science and Department of Psychology, University of Southampton.

Hutchings, GA, Hall, W, Hammond, NV, Kibby, MR, McKnight, C and Riley, D (1992) 'Authoring and evaluation of hypermedia for education', *Computers and Education*, **18**, 171–7.

Ingraham, B and Emery, C (1991) '"France InterActive": a

hypermedia approach to language training', *Educational and Training Technology International*, **28**,4, 321–33.

Jamsa, K (1993) 'Instant Multimedia for Windows 3.1', New York: John Wiley.

Jonassen, DH (1989) *Hypertext/Hypermedia*, Englewood Cliffs, NJ: Educational Technology Publications.

Jonassen, DH and Mandl, HM (1990) *Designing Hypermedia for Learning*, NATO ASI Series F: Computer and Systems Sciences, volume 67, Berlin: Springer-Verlag.

Kibby, MR and Hartley, JR (1992) *Computer-Assisted Learning, Selected Contributions from the CAL '91 Symposium, 8–11 April 1991, Lancaster University*, Oxford: Pergamon Press.

Kibby, MR and Mayes, JT (1989) 'Towards intelligent hypertext', in McAleese, R (ed.) *Hypertext: Theory into Practice*, Oxford: Blackwell.

Kidd, MR, Hutchings, GA, Hall, W and Cesnik, B (1992) 'Applying hypermedia to medical education: an author's perspective', *Educational and Training Technology International*, **29**,2, 143–51.

Knussen, C, Tanner, GR and Kibby, MR (1991) 'An approach to the evaluation of hypermedia', *Computers and Education*, **17**,1, 13–24.

Kommers, PAM, Jonassen, DH and Mayes, JT (1992) *Cognitive Tools for Learning*, NATO ASI Series F: Computer and Systems Sciences, volume 81, Berlin: Springer-Verlag.

Kramlich, D (1984) 'Spatial data management on the USS *Carl Vinson*', *Database Engineering*, **7**,3, 10–19.

Kreitzberg, CB and Shneiderman, B (1992) 'Restructuring knowledge for an electronic encyclopedia', in Harley, J (ed.) *Technology and Writing – Readings in the Psychology of Written Communication*, London: Jessica Kingsley.

Krueger, MW (1991) *Artificial Reality II*, Reading, MA: Addison-Wesley.

Lambert, S and Ropiequet, S (1986) *CD-ROM: The New Papyrus – The Current and Future State of the Art*, Redmond, WA: Microsoft Press.

Landauer, T, Egan, D, Remde, J, Lesk, M, Lochbaum, C and Ketchum, D (1993) 'Enhancing the usability of text through computer delivery and formative evaluation: the SuperBook Project', in McKnight, C, Dillon, A and Richardson, J (eds) *Hypertext: a Psychological Perspective*, Ellis Horwood Series in

Interactive Information Systems, Chichester: Ellis Horwood.

Landow, GP (1989a) 'Hypermedia in literary education, criticism and scholarship', *Computers and the Humanities*, **23**, 173–98.

Landow, GP (1989b) 'The rhetoric of hypertext: some rules for authors', *Journal of Computing in Higher Education*, **1**, 39–64.

Laurel, B (1991) *Computers as Theatre*, Reading, MA: Addison-Wesley.

Lotus (1991) *Outline Specification for 'Lotus Notes'*, Staines: Lotus Development.

McAleese, R (1989) HYPERTEXT: Theory Into Practice, Norwood, NJ: Ablex Publishing Corporation.

McAleese, R and Green, C (1990) (eds) *HYPERTEXT: State of the Art*, Norwood, NJ: Ablex Publishing Corporation.

McCracken, D and Akscyn, RM (1984) 'Experience with the ZOG human-computer interface system', *International Journal of Man-Machine Studies*, **21**, 293–310.

McLellan, H (1992) 'Hyper stories: some guidelines for instructional designers', *Journal of Research on Computing in Education*, **25**,1, 28–49.

McLellan, H (1993) 'Hypertextual Tales: Story Models for Hypertext Design', unpublished manuscript, Department of Educational Technology and Computer Education, Kansas State University.

Martin, J (1990) *Hyperdocuments and How to Create Them*, Englewood Cliffs, NJ: Prentice-Hall.

Mayes, JT, Kibby, MR and Watson, H (1988) 'StrathTutor: the development and evaluation of a learning by browsing system on the Macintosh', *Computers and Education*, **12**,1, 221–9.

Megarry, J (1988) 'Hypertext and compact discs: the challenge of multimedia learning', *British Journal of Educational Technology*, **19**,3, 172–83.

Megarry J (1991) '"Europe in the Round": principles and practice of screen design', *Educational and Training Technology International*, **28**,4, 306–15.

Merrill, MD (1991) 'Constructivism and instructional design', *Educational Technology*, **31**,5, 45–54.

Meyrowitz, N (1986) 'The architecture and construction of an object-orientated hypermedia system and applications framework', *OOPSLA '86 Conference Proceedings*, New York: ACM/

SIGPLAN.

Morrall, A (1991) 'Evaluation of hypertext software to create a public browsing system in a museum', *The Electronic Library*, **9**,4/5, 217–34.

National Instruments (1992) *LabVIEW-2 – the Complete Instrumentation Software System*, Austin, TX: National Instruments Corp.

Negroponte, N (1981) 'Media room', *Proceedings of the Society for Information Display*, **22**,2, 109–13.

Nelson, TH (1967) 'Getting it out of our system' in Schechter, G (ed.) *Information Retrieval: A Critical Review*, Washington, DC: Thompson Books.

Nelson, TH (1980) 'Replacing the printed word: a complete literary system', *IFIP Proceedings*, October.

Noll, J and Scacchi, WW (1991) 'Integrating diverse information repositories: a distributed hypertext approach', *IEEE Computer*, **24**,12, 38–45.

Oren, T, Salomon, G, Kreitman, K and Don, A (1990) 'Guides: characterising the interface', in Laural, B (ed.) *The Art of Human-Computer Interface Design*, Reading, MA: Addison-Wesley.

Pask, G (1976) 'Styles and strategies of learning', *British Journal of Educational Psychology*, **46**, 128–48.

Paterson, P and Adamson, S (1992) 'Cancer information service – a multimedia application designed for the naive user', *The CTISS File*, 14, 30–34.

Pearl, A (1989) 'Sun's link service: a protocol for open linking', in *Proceedings of Hypertext '89*, New York: Association for Computing Machinery.

Philips IMS (1992) *The CD-I Production Handbook*, Wokingham: Addison-Wesley.

Rada, R (1991) *Hypertext: from Text to Expertext*, Maidenhead: McGraw-Hill.

Rada, R (1992) 'Converting a textbook to hypertext', *ACM Transactions on Information Systems*, **10**,3, 294–316.

Raybould, B (1990) 'Solving human performance problems with computers – a case study: building an electronic performance support system', *Performance & Instruction*, 4–14, December.

Richards, S (1993) 'End-User Interfaces to Electronic Books', PhD dissertation, Interactive Systems Research Group, School of Computing and Mathematics, University of Teesside, Cleveland.

Richards, S and Barker, PG (1993) 'Using Hypermedia to Improve the Quality of CBT', paper presented at AETT '92 and updated for submission to the International Journal of Computers in Adult Education and Training.

Richards, S, Barker, PG, Giller, S, Lamont, C and Manji, KA (1991) 'Page structures for electronic books', *Educational and Training Technology International*, **28**,4, 291–305.

Riding, R and Chambers, P (1992) 'CD-ROM versus Textbook: a comparison of the use of two learning media by higher education students', *Educational and Training Technology International*, **29**,4, 342–9.

Ritchie, I (1989) 'HYPERTEXT: moving towards large volumes', *The Computer Journal*, **32**,6, 516–23.

Rockman, S (1992) 'Sony Data Discman DD-IEX', *Personal Computer World*, **15**,3, 262–6.

Rossett, A (1991) 'Electronic job aids', *Data Training*, 24–9, June.

Roth, JP (1991) *Rewritable Optical Storage Technologies*, Westport, CT: Meckler Corporation.

Shafer, DG (1988) *HyperTalk Programming*, Indianapolis, IN: Hayden Books.

Shipman, FM, Chaney, RJ and Gory, GA (1989) 'Distributed hypertext for collaborative research: the Virtual Notebook System', in *Proceedings of Hypertext '89*, New York: Association for Computing Machinery.

Shneiderman, B (1989) 'Reflections on authoring, editing and managing hypertext', in Barrett, G (ed.) *The Society of Text*, Cambridge, MA: MIT Press.

Shneiderman, B (1992a) 'Authoring and editing hypertext', in Hartley, J (ed.) *Technology and Writing – Readings in the Psychology of Written Communication*, London: Jessica Kingsley.

Shneiderman, B (1992b) *Designing the User Interface – Strategies for Effective Human-Computer Interaction*, 2nd edn, Reading, MA: Addison-Wesley Publishing Corporation.

Shneiderman, B and Kearsley, K (1989) *Hypertext Hands-On! – an Introduction to a New Way of Organising and Accessing Information*, Reading, MA: Addison-Wesley.

Siviter, D and Brown, K (1992) 'Hypercourseware', *Computers and Education*, **18**, 163–70.

Smeaton, AF (1991) 'Using hypertext for computer-based learning',

Computers and Education, **17**,3, 173—9.

Subramanian, R and Jambukesan, M (1991) 'Hypermedia: the information system for the 90s', *The Administrator*, **XXXVI**, 97—101.

Tanifuji, S, Tani, M, Yamaashi, K, Tanikoshi, K and Futakawa, M (1993) *HYPERPLANT: Interaction with Plant through Live Video*, Iberaki-ken: Hitachi.

Weatherall, DJ, Ledingham, JGG and Warrell, DA (1989) 'The Oxford Textbook of Medicine on Compact Disc', 2nd edn, Oxford: Oxford University Press.

Whiton, S, Peterson, N and Aiton, J (1992) 'Scenes from the movies: developing extensible multimedia in histology', *The CTISS File*, **14**, 36—40.

Winblad, AL, Edwards, SD and King, DR (1990) *Object-Oriented Software*, Reading, MA: Addison-Wesley.

Woodhead, N (1991) *Hypertext and hypermedia: Theory and Applications*, Wokingham: Addison-Wesley.

Wright, H (1992) 'SGML frees information', *BYTE*, **17**,6, 279—86.

Wright, P (1989) 'Interface alternatives for hypertexts', *Hypermedia*, **1**,2, 146—66.

Yankelovich, N, Meyrowitz, N and van Dam, A (1985) 'Reading and writing the electronic book', *IEEE Computer*, **18**,10, 15—30.

Yankelovich, N, Haan, BT, Meyrowitz, NK and Drucker, SM (1988) 'Intermedia: the concept and the construction of a seamless information environment', *IEEE Computer*, **21**,1, 81—96.

Note: CTISS publications are available from: CTISS, The University of Oxford, 13 Banbury Road, Oxford OX2 6NN.

Index